CW00889270

FRANCIS XAVIER

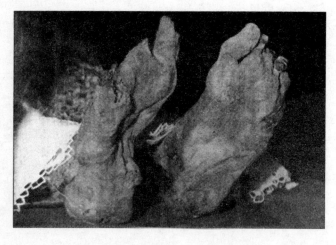

"How beautiful on the mountains
are the feet of one who brings good news."
Is 52:7

Ignatius St Lawrence, SJ

Francis Xavier

ST PAULS

ST PAULS
Morpeth Terrace, London SW1P 1EP, United Kingdom
Moyglare Road, Maynooth, Co. Kildare, London

Copyright © ST PAULS (UK) 1998

ISBN 085439 545 8

Set by TuKan, High Wycombe
Produced in the EC
Printed by The Guernsey Press Co. Ltd., Guernsey, C.I.

ST PAULS is an activity of the priests and brothers of the
Society of St Paul who proclaim the Gospel through the
media of social communication

Contents

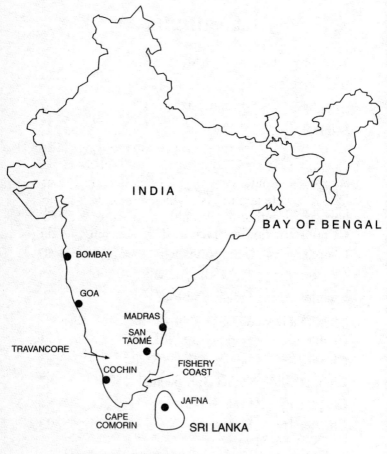

INDIA

BAY OF BENGAL

BOMBAY

GOA

MADRAS

SAN
TAOMÉ

TRAVANCORE

COCHIN

FISHERY
COAST

JAFNA

CAPE
COMORIN

SRI LANKA

INDIAN OCEAN

Introduction

In 1990 I wrote a life of St Ignatius Loyola[1] which was well received. The present book is an account of his best friend, Francis Xavier.[2] As I did in *Ignatius*, I have tried to appeal to both younger readers and to adults who would appreciate a brief and simple outline of the life and ideals of Xavier. Francis was not himself an author – his only 'work' was a manuscript instruction to go with his preaching of the faith. However, he did write numerous letters, mainly describing his mission: the journeys, methods of explaining his teaching, obstacles (and there were many) which he had to overcome, his joys and sorrows – to instance a few subjects. A great number of these letters have been preserved and they provided me with a main source. I have also drawn on some modern lives in English, but I have never visited the lands of

---

1. *Ignatius, Founder of the Jesuits*. ST PAULS Publishing, 1990.
2. In English the word 'Xavier' is pronounced as though it rhymes with 'saviour', with the accent on the first syllable. In Spanish, the 'x' becomes a 'j' (pronounced 'h'), and the word is pronounced as though it rhymes with 'have-ee-air', with the accent on the last syllable.

the apostolate in the East. I hope that this omission will not take too much from my story.

My warm thanks go to those, both Jesuit and Lay, who have read and commented on the text. Opinions and corrections from any of my readers will help to inform me if I have done Francis Xavier credit.

IGNATIUS ST LAWRENCE, SJ

CHAPTER 1

Mission Accepted

"Of course I accept – I'll get ready at once. I've been praying for years for a chance to be sent to the Indies, thank you, thank you." With these words Francis Xavier gave himself to an adventure which was to bring extraordinary results in the years ahead for himself and for the Church. He was speaking to his best friend and fellow-Basque, Ignatius Loyola, in the small house where they were living in Rome. Both belonged to a new Religious Order,* the Jesuits, whose founder and leader, Ignatius, now aged 49, was explaining to Francis, aged 34, the mission he was giving him.

"Francis, you know that King John of Portugal has asked the Pope for some of us Jesuits to be sent to his possessions in the Indies to reinforce the European priests already there."

"I do know this: why are you telling me again?"

"Because, Francis, apart from you and me, there

_____

* See the end of this chapter for an explanation of this and related terms.

are only two Jesuits available, as the rest of us are already working for the Pope."

"I know that too," answered Francis, "and you have appointed them, Simon and Nicholas."

"There's the problem," said Ignatius, "Nicholas has fallen ill and will not be fit to travel."

"Why not? He will surely be better soon?"

"Soon is too late: the man must be ready to set off tomorrow on the journey to Lisbon – that is the starting point for sailing to the Indies. Do you accept?"… Silence… "Francis, I'm appointing you, do you accept?"…

The next day, 15th March 1540, they said their goodbyes. They were never to meet again.

* * *

How had these two come together in Rome in the first place?

Ignatius (born in 1491 and baptised Inigo) belonged to a noble family whose home was the castle of Loyola in one of the Basque provinces in the Pyrenean mountains of north-west Spain. In youth and early manhood he had been trained in the service of the King of Spain, partly at Court and partly in defending the country against invasion. He was absorbed in pageantry, romance, fine clothes, amusement and women, with the ambition of making a distinguished marriage with a lady of high rank. He was also immensely proud of his skill as a man of action, a knight, in tournaments, duels and battle.

At the age of thirty a badly wounded knee had put an end to his career as a soldier and left him slowly recovering for nine months. In his boredom he started reading the only books available – the Life of Christ and the Lives of the Saints – not the type of books he had enjoyed so far. Yet, as he read, he was awoken to a new ambition, for Christ and the saints seemed to challenge him to take up a fresh life, a nobler kind of service than that of a knight or courtier. He now planned to become a poor man, anxious to face hardship in bringing the Gospel to unbelievers, and regarding it an honour to be humble and despised in such a cause.

After a brief pilgrimage to the Holy Land, he returned to Europe at the age of 33, determined to start studying to become a priest (a 'late vocation'), and for this he chose the University of Paris. By now he had developed as a man of character, a natural leader, with a shrewd knowledge of people and of the world, a great desire to help his neighbour, and an attractive manner of speaking about the things of God. As he studied he was looking for fellow-students whom he might inspire to share his ideals and future life. Gradually a group formed round him made up of fellow-Basques – Francis Xavier and five others – from the French Alps, Spain and Portugal.

Francis (born in 1506) came from the castle of Xavier in the Basque province of Navarre, some 60 miles south-east of Loyola. His own youth did not have the varied and exciting life of Ignatius', but he had formed two overriding ambitions. The first was to have it officially proved that his family, by name Jassu, was descended from the kings and queens of Navarre. The second was to qualify himself for a high-ranking post in the Church.

It was this latter need which took him to the University of Paris at the age of 19, already a young man of robust build and personal charm.

Four years later he found himself sharing lodgings with Ignatius and the student from the French Alps, Peter Favre. Francis did not take to his fellow-countryman at first, for he could not appreciate why this 'old man' was leading a student life and why this once proud noble had turned beggar for enough money to cover his fees and lodging. Francis' own tastes in student life were sport (athletics), parties and women – not unlike those of Ignatius when in his early 20s. But Ignatius saw in Francis qualities which convinced him that he was just the sort of companion he was looking for. Quite possibly, Ignatius reflected, as he had changed from a life dominated by worldly ambitions, so he could steer Francis in the same direction. He took his time in winning him over, partly by contributing some of his income from begging to Francis when he became hard up, partly by giving him wise advice on how to avoid the dangers of social life in the university. That Ignatius' method was successful is shown by Francis' words in a letter to his own brother a year or so later – that he would never be able to repay the debt he owed to Ignatius.

In Francis and Ignatius two enthusiasts met, two men of chivalry, their ambitions transformed into a search for God's guidance in their future lives. The story of how they and the other companions developed from university students into Jesuit priests, so that Ignatius could give Francis the mission to India, will be revealed later. Meanwhile, the first stage of Francis' many journeys must now be told…

…The route to Lisbon is easily described: north from Rome to the Alps, then west across southern France almost to the Atlantic, south over the Pyrenees and on through north-west Spain, and so to Portugal.

Francis did not travel alone, but as a member of

the escort of the Portuguese Ambassador returning to visit his country. Although in his youth Francis had grown accustomed to riding everywhere, he had, since joining Ignatius and his companions, learnt to walk, even on long journeys, as befitted a poor man. However, on this particular expedition he had no choice but to ride, if only to keep up with the 'caravan'. Following a spell of very poor health in Rome (so poor that people thought he had not long to live) he seemed to come to life again. He was to the fore in the rescue of fellow-travellers from fast-flowing rivers or steep ravines, and as a member of the group he showed the talents which were to attract others wherever he went: enthusiasm, courtesy, hard work, charm. "You can't help liking him," they would say, "he puts you at your ease, he seems to cast a spell on you." When not helping in rescue work he might be found grooming the horses, or in a quiet spot hearing a man's confession.

A fortnight later after the departure from Rome came the first stop, at Bologna. Here Francis was surprised to be given a great welcome. Many Catholics still remembered the time, two years before, when he had been working in one of the parishes soon after his ordination as a priest. He had impressed the people by his devout manner of celebrating the Eucharist, the long hours he would spend in the confessional, his visits to the sick and prisoners, and the amount of time he gave to his private prayers. There was also the easy way he had of talking about God – it went straight to the heart and moved his hearers to sorrow for their sins and the desire to lead a better life. In Bologna a letter from Ignatius caught him up, and in his reply Francis spoke of the kindness of the Ambassador and of his concern that all his officials should go to confession and holy communion at Easter. His next letter to Ignatius was not until the arrival in Lisbon, three months and 2,000 miles later. In it he gave no details of weather, scenery or places visited en route – he merely mentioned the great toil and hardship.

As the travellers crossed from France into Spain at the western end of the Pyrenees, Francis was in his homeland – the Basque region. The Basques are a unique people, neither French nor Spanish (their lands are partly in each country), who speak a very difficult language of their own.

Francis, the youngest member of the ancient noble family of Xavier and Jassu (he had three sisters and two brothers), was born in the castle of Xavier in Holy Week on 7th April 1506, and was baptised in the church which his parents had built near the castle. The loyalty of the family to the Catholic faith was passed on to Francis throughout his boyhood. One of the most touching survivals from earlier times is the life-size wooden figure of Christ on the Cross (thirteenth century). It is called the 'Smiling Christ' from the way in which our Lord's lips are parted, and to this day still hangs in a tiny chapel in the castle.

Xavier is in Navarre, about 60 miles south-east of Bilbao (Ignatius' home in Loyola is about the same distance north of Xavier). As castles go, Xavier is small and looks over a parched, rolling landscape, watered by mountain torrents, beneath vast skies, with blazing hot summers and terrible winters.

Whilst Francis was growing up, his brothers were often away from home, fighting in various campaigns on behalf of the kingdom of Navarre, and he would constantly hear of their exploits, although too young to join in them. His education was patchy: some school work in Spanish and Latin, training in etiquette, horsemanship and sport. The travels and labours of his later life showed what a strong constitution he had. To this was added a delightful charm of manner and intense determination, a hallmark of the Basque race.

In spite of the rush at the beginning of his journey (we remember that Francis had only one day in which to get ready), the Ambassador and his company did not eventually arrive in Lisbon until June (1540). By then the fleet for that year had already sailed, so that Francis had to wait for the next boat – 10 months later!

Early on, he and Simon Rodrigues, one of the two original choices, were given the chance of an audience with King John, who questioned them closely about this new Order of priests to which they both belonged, for the two of them were the first members of the 'Society (or Company) of Jesus' to be seen in Portugal.

In Lisbon they found much pastoral work to do: confessions, counselling, preaching, retreats. They were so well liked that within a few months there was a move to keep them in Lisbon for good, on the grounds that they would be much more valuable working to revive the faith of Catholics in Portugal than they would be amongst non-Christians in the Indies. When told by letter of this, Ignatius suggested to King John that he keep one in Lisbon and send the other to the Indies. Simon, then, who was Portuguese, remained in his country, whilst Francis was instructed to be ready to sail towards the end of March (1541). He would have as companions two fellow-Jesuits, Francis Mansilhas, not yet a priest, and a young Italian priest, Micer Paul.

In his farewell letter to Ignatius on March 18th, Francis mentioned that at his last audience with the King, the latter had spoken of his great unhappiness when thinking of the state of non-Christians in India, their ignorance of the true God, their many sins and his own pleasure at Francis' mission to evangelize them. The letter went on: "The King is sending us with many gifts (to present to local rulers in India). He has also asked the new Viceroy, Martin de Sousa, with whom we shall be travelling, to give us special treatment on his ship, the *Santiago*. This he proposes to do personally, looking after our needs and inviting us to his table." Francis in fact was very easy to satisfy, wanting only a few books and "a woollen cloak to use during the wild weather near the Cape of Good Hope". He refused a personal servant, intending to look after his clothes himself. Towards the end of this letter Francis writes, "I do not know if we shall ever see each other again in this life because of the great distance between Rome and India, so let us pray God to unite us in the next life."

The five ships in the fleet – the Viceroy's flagship of 700 tons and four smaller ones – were held up in port for a fortnight by strong Atlantic gales and could not sail until April 7th, the very day of Francis' 35th birthday. On board were 700 people: the Viceroy and his officials, rich merchants, many soldiers, men looking for fortunes or adventures in India, slaves from Africa, criminals. No women were taken. One of the *Lives* of Francis Xavier describes the start: "The day of departure was one of anxiety and sadness for the people of Lisbon, at the thought of the dangers of the journey. Many prayers and Masses were said, and many went to confession for what might be the last time, whilst some made their wills." Francis' own last act was to preach on the shore. Then the ships moved off, watched by the whole population to the blare of trumpets and chant of hymns.

NOTES

Religious Order/Institute: a group approved by the competent Church authority who live in community and profess the public vows of poverty, chastity and obedience. A Religious Institute may be of Diocesan right (mainly under the authority of the local bishop) or of Pontifical right (for the most part under the direct authority of the Pope). It may be clerical (founded to be engaged in the work of ordained ministry) or lay (founded for a number of works, but excluding that of the ordained ministry) or mixed (constituted of clerics and lay members). It may be contemplative (devoted mainly to the pursuit of prayer and contemplation) or active (given to the works of apostolate). Each institute is regulated and governed by Canon Law and the institute's own constitutions approved by the competent Church authority.

Religious life: a way of living the Christian life that includes communal living and the profession of public (solemn or simple) vows of poverty, chastity and obedience in a community approved by the competent Church authority. Religious life has a rich history of development that produced various models, many of which continue today. The forms include (1) the monastic life, in which the community lives together and is bound by the celebration of the Liturgical Hours; (2) the mendicant life, which was established to give members more mobility to preach the gospel where needed; (3) apostolic communities (contemplatives in action), which maintain a major focus on apostolic works. Religious life embraces communities given to the works of the apostolate (preaching and pastoral activity, teaching, nursing, publishing, foreign missions, social work, etc.) as well as communities devoted solely to prayer and contemplation.

Religious: a member of a Religious Institute (Order/Congregation) i.e., a group of individuals who live life together as brothers or sisters and publicly profess the evangelical counsels of poverty, chastity and obedience – here religious vows.

The Jesuits – Origin: At the end of their university days Ignatius, Francis and the other five companions chose to remain together as friends. They had all made Ignatius' Spiritual Exercises and wanted to be ordained as priests, go to the Holy Land, settle there and imitate our Lord's way of life. However, there was at this time no chance of sailing (from Venice to Palestine) since the Turks controlled the seapassage. This setback did not dampen the enthusiasm of the companions, and they re-thought their future. This resulted in a visit to the Pope (Paul III), when they asked him to grant them tasks to carry out for the Church: they were ready to go anywhere. The Pope was delighted to accept their offer, and was soon sending them to different parts of Italy. He also asked for a written summary of their way of life and their objectives, to enable him to make up his mind whether the companions could, as a group of their own, become known as what is called a Religious Order.

The central part of the summary ran, "We have chosen to be called the 'Companions of Jesus' and to fight under the flag of the Cross in the service of God in the Church. We will vow to be poor, chaste and humble, as Christ was, and to go wherever the Pope may send us, in Europe or overseas, to defend and spread the true Faith. We will do this by preaching, teaching (including teaching children their Religion), the Spiritual Exercises, by Mass and the Sacraments. We also want to work for those in prisons or hospitals and any others who are in need of help. We will carry out all our tasks free of charge."

The Pope's official permission took more than a year to come, but what did come in the meantime was the request mentioned at the beginning of Chapter I for two companions to answer the call of King John of Portugal.

The Spiritual Exercises: a small book, consisting not of a collection of sermons or chapters on spiritual topics, but of a series of subjects about which to meditate, or pray in some other way, in order to find out what God wants of us. Much of the book is guidance and suggestions about prayer and the way to plan a new life (based on Ignatius' experiences). For each subject he gives a simple scheme and usually chooses a passage from the Gospel; this he does not explain in detail, for he wants the retreat-maker to discover for themselves how this part of Christ's life can help them in their own needs. At various stages Ignatius brings in a meditation of his own, e.g. on sin, on the following of Christ the King, or on the methods of Satan. The whole is preparing a person to make a deliberate choice about how to serve God better in the future. The 'full' Exercises are spread over about a month.

The Jesuits – Progress: From their foundation onwards the Jesuits' numbers (originally limited to 60) continued to increase in many countries and several continents for the next two centuries and more. Then came a crisis in 1773, when Pope Clement XIV, under heavy pressure and threats from several European governments (who did not like the Order), abolished them as an Order.

However, some 40 years later, early in the nineteenth century, Europe was a different place, and the then Pope, Pius VII, brought the Order to life again. For the rest of the century and for most of this one there has been a steady increase in numbers and activities, with special emphasis on foreign missions. Since the Second Vatican Council (in the 1960s) the Order has defined its purpose as 'the service of faith and the promotion of the justice of the Gospel'. A particular modern activity has focused on the care of refugees through the Jesuit Refugee Service.

At the time of writing, the Order numbers about 22,000 (not unlike the total when they were abolished). There are branches in at least 119 countries.

Jesuits and Education: Many regard the Jesuits as mainly concerned with education. In fact, education in the sense of running their own schools or colleges, was not a work which Ignatius had in mind at the beginning. He supposed that his companions would need to be free to move from one job to another and not be tied down by occupying particular buildings. But there soon came a popular demand for the Order to open schools, colleges and even universities. Hence, Ignatius recognised this as a sign of the times and followed it. At the time of the 450th anniversary of the Order's foundation an estimate spoke of one-and-a-half million students and pupils worldwide in 56 countries.

Chapter 2

At Sea

The route from Lisbon was south, along the west coast of Africa, round the Cape of Good Hope, north up the east coast and finally veering east to reach the chief Portuguese city in India, Goa, several hundred miles south of modern Bombay.

When Francis wrote his next letter to Rome, nine months later, the fleet had still not reached India. "I was sea sick for the first two months", were his opening words. This was hardly surprising, since he had never been at sea before – all the travels we know about had been by land. They were: Xavier to Paris (1525), Paris to Venice (1536), Venice to Rome (1538), Rome to Lisbon (1540). Apart from the trial of sea-sickness there were many other hardships: poor food and foul water, disease (often leading to death), poverty of many of the passengers. Further perils were caused by the weather, by shoals and reefs, and the danger of pirates. There were the 'doldrums' – a period of about 40 days when the ships were becalmed in the latitude of the equator, since they could only progress by sailing *with* the wind (there was no way in which such large vessels could be rowed).

One traveller has written: "Forty days on a windless ocean in tropical heat brought enormous strain on the nerves, health and tempers of the passengers, and caused much of the food supplies to go putrid. At times conditions were made even worse by sudden fierce thunderstorms or cruel warm rain. Below deck the atmosphere was like that of a red hot oven; on deck every inch was occupied by passengers and frequent were the disputes and knife-fights over the right to have a few square feet of shade." Francis had been given his own space, a cabin towards the stern, and he was a guest at the Viceroy's table for meals. However, he did not think of these luxuries as his own, for he was always on the lookout for sick or starving passengers. The sick he put in his own bed (himself sleeping on deck); the starving he either fed with his own helpings from the Viceroy's table, or provided them with what he could induce the better-off passengers to hand over (himself surviving on leftovers).

Francis was not a doctor, but he nursed the sick by washing them and their clothes, dosing them and emptying their commodes. Furthermore, he would comfort the dying, hear their confessions, give them the last rites and say the final prayers when they were buried at sea. Those who saw him at work marvelled at how cheerful, friendly and courteous he always was. He also made himself at home with the other passengers: joining the soldiers for a game of dice, or discussing the price of pepper with the merchants, and once even taking the helm when the pilot fell asleep. His own terse summing-up of the voyage was, "…as for myself, the hardships were of such a kind that otherwise I would not have faced them for a single day for the whole world."

To resume our account of Francis' journey: in August 1541 the fleet was forced to wait again. The two weeks lost before leaving Lisbon, added to the 40 days in the doldrums, led to their being unable to sail up the east coast of Africa in the face of the monsoons. Hence, they put in at Mozambique, on the south-east African coast, 15 degrees south of the equator, and described as "small, low-lying, with very unhealthy air, but well-suited for ships and crews to spend time resting after the difficult passage round the Cape of Good Hope". It also provided a welcome change of diet with a choice of oranges, apples, lemons, bananas and fresh meat.

After some months there Francis wrote a long letter to Ignatius and other companions in Rome, relating part of the story of the voyage so far. Others may have rested but Francis was busier than ever, living in the local hospital and caring for the sick of all five ships in the fleet, as well as any who fell ill during the wait. After a time he wore himself out and had to be looked after by the Santiago's surgeon, who 'bled' him nine times and reported that he had been delirious for three days. Francis' letter to Rome ended, "I would love to be able to go on writing to you, but at present sickness makes this impossible. I am middling well, thanks be to God." What he did not mention, although others noticed the fact, was that the number of men who died on the voyage was much lower than usual. Many gave credit for this 'miracle' to Francis' devoted nursing of the sick. "Everyone held him for a saint", was the opinion of the ship's surgeon.

In February 1542 the Viceroy grew impatient and decided that he and his colleagues would go ahead to Goa, using a rather unseaworthy vessel, the *Coulam*, thereby risking attacks from Turkish pirates. The ship kept close to land until it reached the approaches to the Red Sea where lies the island of Socotra, an unexciting place, whose main product was dates. Francis, who had been taken away from the hospital in Mozambique, found much to do in Socotra. On landing, he learnt that the people claimed that their ancestors had been converted to Christianity by the Apostle Thomas. They were able to recite many Christian prayers by heart, but without understanding their meaning, nor had any of them been baptised. Francis put this right by baptising many of them including babies, in return for which he was touched to receive a gift of dates! This island was another spot which he left with reluctance, but the Viceroy would hear nothing of him staying, saying that India was a far more important part of the world. Although he did not stay, Francis never forgot Socotra, for he later planned to send Jesuit priests there, and he also asked for the King's support. But the idea came to nothing, and all the people of Socotra became Moslems and remain so to this day.

The last stage of the voyage was speeded up by favourable winds, and Francis landed at Goa in May 1542, two years and two months after saying farewell to Ignatius. In honour of the new Viceroy, church bells rang, cannons roared and triumphal arches were built.

Chapter 3

Journey's End – Goa

The 'India' where Francis landed and later worked was a very small part of the whole, from the southern tip of the country as far north as the latitude of the modern city of Chennai (Madras). It is hard to find Goa on the map, for it is neither so large nor so important as it was in the sixteenth century (in its most flourishing stage it was known as 'Golden Goa'). The city was situated on the west coast, south of modern Murnbai, but nothing remains from Francis' time, for mosquitoes eventually made the place so unhealthy that it was evacuated and rebuilt some miles away (where the town of Panjim now rests). The only buildings standing nowadays on the site of Francis' Goa are the cathedral and Jesuit basilica of Bom (Good) Jesus, built about 50 years after his death as a resting place for his body.

What was Goa like to look at and live in? One comparison is that of Lisbon, the second largest city in Europe after Paris, for the Portuguese copied the architecture of their own capital. In a letter to Rome Francis wrote, "Goa is a sight to be seen, for it is wholly Christian, with many Franciscan friars, a cathedral of much distinction, as well as many other churches." Not many years later, a French traveller said, "The city is walled with towers and great Guns to hinder the slaves from running away... There are several Religious Orders and the Jesuits have five 'public houses'." One other writer declared Goa to be 'Rome in India.'

Francis did not elaborate on the history of Goa before Portuguese rule, even if he knew it. Most recently the city had been occupied by Moslems, who found the harbour to be a convenient starting-place for pilgrimage to Mecca: earlier it was for 1000 years a Hindu city. About the time of Francis' birth, the Portuguese admiral, Albuquerque, captured it from the Moslems with great slaughter of the population, destruction of mosques and burning alive of prisoners.

Goa was valuable to the Portuguese as a market for cargoes from further east to be sent on to Europe: gold, spices (especially cloves, pepper, cinnamon and nutmeg), pearls, tortoiseshell. In exchange it received from Europe: silver, munitions, wine, cheese and oil. All these were carried in Portuguese, not Muslim ships.

Before getting to know the city, Francis, who already knew the new Viceroy, wanted to visit the Archbishop, another member of the Albuquerque family. The latter had never heard of Jesuits, and asked Francis to explain who they were. Then he asked, "Fr Francis, who sent you to India, and why?"

"Your Grace," he replied, "His Holiness, the Pope, is responsible, for he heard from King John how badly more priests were needed in India, and asked my Superior, Ignatius, to choose two of us companions for this task. I and another, Simon, were selected, and we made ready for the journey, but Simon was kept back in Lisbon by the King."

"Did the King or the Pope tell what you were to do here?"

"My main task is to help the Christians, and to teach the native population and any others who want to become Christians. Therefore your Grace, I put myself in your hands – you will know best."

"Father, I welcome you with all my heart, you will never be short of work here, for I have very few priests left for Mass, preaching and the sacraments." Francis went on, "The Pope has appointed me as his Nuncio (Ambassador) in the East, and given me certain powers: I will consult you before I use them."

"Use your powers, I can trust you; you will be too far away for any consultation."

There was in fact a special task awaiting Francis, but the weather prevented him from sailing at once. This was the monsoon season, from early June onwards, when the temperature drops, heavy rain falls, perhaps for two days at a time, enough to irrigate the paddy-fields for sowing. Preparations are made to store up rice and fruit – and to make sure that umbrellas are ready, especially around Goa, where the rainfall is abundant in quantity compared with most of the rest of India.

Meanwhile Francis immediately found work to do in Goa and based himself at the hospital – one of many which the Portuguese were building in Africa and Asia for the benefit of both Christians and non-Christians. He was at the service of those injured at sea and of the dying. The Governor of the hospital once said, "I am amazed at Fr Francis – he does a hard day's work, and then, instead of going to bed, he lies on the floor beside the most dangerously ill patient so as to be able to help him at a moment's notice. He sleeps so lightly that the least moan of a patient will rouse him and send him like a flash to help the suffering person."

After a morning in the hospital for Mass, holy communion and confession, he would visit the three prisons of Goa, described by one ex-prisoner as "places reeking with infection, where up to two or three hundred slaves, galley-birds and other scum are herded together anyhow". To Francis these were simply people in need. Next, he would be off begging – not for himself, but on behalf of the sick, the prisoners and the lepers – whatever the weather, ready with his umbrella to shelter him from the sun, rain or waterspouts. He gradually became a familiar sight in the slave-market, at the merchants' stalls or in the houses, of the wealthy, making full use of his charm.

Francis also made time to help those who were not prisoners, nor sick, but in normal health. It was spiritual help he was offering by teaching them more about their Christian faith. He gathered young people together in the small chapel of Our Lady near the hospital, by going through the streets, ringing a little bell and proclaiming, "Christians, for the love of God send your sons and daughters, your slaves, men and women, for Christian teaching." Soon a procession formed, and once in the chapel they saw and heard him preach: so intent were they that they sometimes imitated his vivid actions and words. Eventually, he taught them hymns whose words contained the teachings of the Church, or made up a kind of litany whose responses formed an act of faith. These words were simple, and the catchy melodies could have been those he learnt in his own youth.

In a letter to the Jesuits in Rome he wrote, "On Sundays and Feast days after the noon meal I preach on parts of the Creed to the native Indian Christians, then I teach them the prayers, 'Our Father' and so on. In the mornings I have been outside the city at the leper-colony: the lepers are very attached to me." This was no surprise, for he used to call them 'my friends' – not a word usually used for lepers.

September was the time for writing these letters: the monsoon was over and ships for Europe were preparing to sail. To the details just mentioned Francis added an account of a college being built in the city to train young men for the priesthood. "The College", he wrote, "is for the natives from other lands, of different tribes and nationalities to be taught the faith and then return to their homes to spread it. It already has 60 boys with a priest as rector. I believe that in six years it will have more than 300 pupils. The Viceroy is writing for more Jesuits to come and teach, including a Latin master." The College was called by some 'St Paul's' and by others 'Holy Faith' (in later years, all Jesuits in India were called 'Paulists' from their connection with the college).

CHAPTER 4

The Pearl Fishers

With the sailing season starting, Francis was now able to travel to the destination which had been planned for him originally – a journey of about 600 miles south-east from Goa to the very tip of India, Cape Comorin. Turning round this cape and travelling north-east he reached the territory of the Paravas, called by the Portuguese the 'Fishery Coast'. A recent writer describes the area as follows. "It is a hot, barren strip of coast, mostly of sand (and therefore no good for crops) between the sea and more fertile land further west. Every so often there are oases, studded with palmyra palms, and on these, supplemented by fish and rice, about 30,000 natives eke out an existence. The whole area is smaller than an English county like Surrey."

The main 'income' of these natives was derived, not from fish to eat, but from pearl oysters. The fishermen and boys dived naked with just a net to collect the oysters containing the pearls, and a knife to deal with sharks. March was the diving season, and the pearls were sold to merchants who offered a low price, and then sold them on at a great profit.

Part of the annual catch was reserved for the Queen of Portugal to adorn her slippers. Francis is said to have written to the Queen, suggesting that, as an act of charity, she should allow the Paravas to keep for themselves her share of the pearl harvest, a request which she graciously granted. Sadly many of the divers suffered in later years from lung disease caused by holding their breath for so long under water (no scubas in those days).

The Paravas had in fact been 'converted' to Christianity not many years before, but had not been able to practise their new religion simply because there were not enough priests to instruct them. Francis' letter to Rome explains, "The Christians here were baptised eight years ago, but owing to their having no priest to celebrate Mass for them and teach them the prayers, they know nothing whatever of their religion except to say that they are Christians. Immediately after I disembarked on the coast, I went off to the various villages where they lived and baptised all the children who had not yet received the sacrament, as well as a large number of babies. The children besieged me in such numbers that I had no time to say my Office nor sleep. They clamoured to be taught some prayers, and I began to understand the words 'suffer the little children to come to me, for such is the Kingdom of Heaven'."

Francis quickly came up against he problem of what language to use. He explained, "...since they did not understand me nor I them, their native tongue being Tamil and mine Basque, I assembled individuals who understood both Portuguese and Tamil. After they had helped me with the great toil for many days we translated the prayers into Tamil, that is: the Sign of the Cross, the Commandments, the 'Our Father',

31

'Hail Mary', 'Hail Holy Queen', the 'I Confess'. I then learned them by heart, went through the entire village with a bell and assembled all the boys and men: we had a lesson twice a day. Within the space of a month the boys knew the prayers, so I told them to teach their parents and all those in the house what they had learnt."

Francis makes it all sound fairly simple, but he does say "great toil for many days". Learning the translations by heart would not be too difficult for intelligent children, but it was an enormous effort for a man in his late thirties, on top of all his other activities. Two passages from his letter well describe how full and tiring each day was: "There is such a great multitude of those who are being converted... that it frequently happens that my arms become exhausted from baptising, and I can no longer speak from having recited the prayers in their language. There are days when I baptise an entire village, and on the coast where I now am there are 30 Christian villages." Again, "There were so many who asked me to go to their homes, recite some prayers over their sick... that the mere reading of the Gospels, teaching the boys, answering their questions, burying the dead, leaves me no time for anything else. So I leave a teacher in each village to continue what I have begun, and order those who know how to write to copy the prayers and then assemble everyone on Sundays to recite them."

Thereupon Francis never ceased in his letters to beseech the authorities in Europe to send more priests. A passage in one letter became famous: "What a multitude of gentiles would become Christians if only there were priests to help them... Perhaps some of the learned men of Europe would think whether they are using their talents properly, and perhaps they might shout to God and ask him to show them what to do – even to volunteer for the Indies." In his reply (received more than a year later) Ignatius said, "When your letters arrive in Rome, they are translated, copied and read by young and old, not only in Rome, but in other countries too." The result was just what Francis wanted – many more applying to become priests for the Indies.

For a whole year Francis travelled to and fro, up and down the 140 miles of coastline, visiting all 30 villages more than once. One account of his journeys gives us some idea of what they were like. "Walking in the hot season was like mile after mile on live coals, and in the rainy season like floundering through a sea of mud. High winds brought with them vast clouds of grit and dust. Animals and other living creatures could include poisonous snakes of every kind, crocodiles and pythons, jackals, bandicoot rats, vampire bats, not to mention tigers and leopards."

At journey's end each day the evening meal would be the same: rice… rice… sometimes rice with fish… no bread, no vegetable, no meat, no wine. A native who often saw Francis once said, "He would sometimes go two days eating only a few morsels. As for sleep, three hours was often all he snatched." Other people noticed that he spent his night praying, "as often as not under the stars".

In the autumn of 1543 he went back to Goa to report on what he had been doing. Here he found a thrilling surprise awaiting him – a letter from Rome, only the second since he left Lisbon over two years before. In it he learnt from Ignatius that six months after Francis' departure, the Jesuits had been officially approved by the Pope, that Ignatius had been elected leader (Father General) and that his companions had all pronounced their vows as members of the Order. Francis now did the same in the presence of the Archbishop of Goa, and thus was able to put SJ after his name. He then wrote out in his own hand the words of the vows, and kept the parchment round his neck to remind him of what he had promised. With this he put the signature of Ignatius, cut out from his letter. His reply to Ignatius contained the information quoted above about his activities with the Paravas.

CHAPTER 5

Persecution

Francis returned to his converts, taking with him three helpers (none of them priests from Europe yet), men who would be able to organise the villages, help people in times of trouble and start building churches. Speaking about himself at this time he said, "I have been ill with fever for five days and I've been bled twice. Before that I was eight days at sea. God alone knows what I had to suffer on that voyage. I sometimes wish that I could escape from all these troubles."

He noticed that the Paravas were not kindly treated by their Portuguese fellow-Christians who used them as slaves whom they could buy or carry off as they liked. Francis exploded, "How can we expect these Indians to be attracted by Christianity, when Christians themselves set such a terrible example?"

He was soon to come to the rescue of his Paravas in quite another way. They were being pillaged and attacked by a certain war-like tribe from further north – the Badagas – who saw newly converted Paravas as friends of the hated Portuguese. The villagers were either massacred by swift-moving cavalry or put to flight, many dying of hunger, thirst or exposure. Some put out in their fishing boats to take refuge on rocky islands off the coast, whilst on land more and more refugees made their way as far south as possible to Cape Comorin (the 'tip' of India) where Francis was.

The Paravas had no defence against further raids – except the bravery of Francis. One night, when a sudden raid occurred, he interrupted his prayer and walked alone straight towards the enemy. Something in what they saw about this solitary man made them rein their horses, turn around and flee. Francis then spent his time going from village to village along the coast collecting food, clothes and other supplies for those marooned on the rocks, and then supervised the cargoes being loaded onto boats.

As the raids ceased, Francis was free to start preaching to another tribe, the Macaus, who stretched north-west from Cape Comorin, an area called Travancore, one of whose rulers had encouraged Francis to come – this was in November 1544. He claimed later that within a single month he baptised more than 10,000 persons! He explained, "After baptism I give each one his name in writing (on a palm leaf); the men then return to their homes and send their wives and families. When I have finished baptising I order them to destroy the huts in which they keep their idols and I have them break the idols into tiny pieces since they are now Christians."

Before he had finished the instruction of this tribe, Francis received news about another group of recent converts – the Careas. They lived in an area on the east coast further north than the Paravas, where the mainland practically touches the north-west coast of Sri Lanka (Ceylon), part of the kingdom of Jaffna. It was not Francis himself, but one of his helpers who had answered the call of the natives (who may well have heard about Christianity from their fellow fishermen, the Paravas).

In a matter of weeks the unnamed missionary had instructed and baptised around 1,000 Careas. Although in Travancore the ruler had encouraged Francis, here in Sri Lanka the Hindu Rajah, Sankily, was enraged at the thought of his subjects coming under Portuguese influence, and ordered the new Christians to give up their faith or be put to death. No less than 600 disobeyed, were tortured and massacred, thus becoming the first martyrs of the Indies.

Francis' reactions were both of great joy at the fidelity of the converts and immense fury at the savage cruelty of Sankily. He felt that if this could be done to one group of Christians then all others might be at risk. He lost no time in embarking to look for the Viceroy (somewhere in the Goa region) and demand that he take action by severely punishing Sankily. The Viceroy was so distressed that he ordered a large fleet to be equipped to capture and destroy Sankily. Francis was more than satisfied, but thought that it would be enough to teach the offender a lesson rather than destroy him. In the end neither happened – the Viceroy could not afford to fall out with Sankily, and Francis waited in vain for the promised fleet.

Unable to do any more, Francis now began to think of leaving India and moving south-east towards Malaya, and still further east to the Indonesian Archipelago. "I have heard", he said, "that in the islands called Macular the natives are well-disposed for the service of God; the king of one of them sent for priests. As I was originally sent to the Indies, not just to India itself, I am going to take this invitation seriously. I will spend the month of May (1545) finding out more and making up my mind whether God wants *me* to go. There are now enough priests for the Christians of southern India – or there soon will be – which leaves me free to think of moving on."

CHAPTER 6

New Horizons

To "get away from it all" Francis chose to sail to San Thomé, a small town of Portuguese and native Christians, 160 miles further up the coast from the pearl-fishers, near the modern Madras. The name of the town is simply the Portuguese for 'St Thomas'. There was a centuries-old tradition that Thomas, the Apostle, had preached, been martyred and been buried there, his tomb being in a church which has been rebuilt several times and is now a cathedral. The existence of native Christians in the area goes back to the third or fourth century. There were still some there when Portuguese explorers and merchants arrived in the early sixteenth century, 30 years before Francis' visit.

The ship on which he sailed had to give up the journey after twice being practically wrecked. Francis then walked, in the deadly heat of May, and on arrival introduced himself to the priest in the town, Fr Gaspar, who made room for his guest in his small cottage near the church. For the next four weeks Francis was neither travelling nor hard at work instructing his converts. He was able to relax, making what is nowadays called a 'retreat', in order – by his prayers – to find out whether God really wanted him to go to Indonesia. He decided that he should go and prepare for the month's voyage of about 1,500 miles across the Bay of Bengal and beyond, to the port of Malacca in Malaya (approximately 60 miles north-west of modern Singapore), whence ships left for the Macassar islands.

The letters he wrote before and after the voyage are worth quoting: BEFORE – "If no Portuguese ships are sailing this year for Malacca, I shall go on a Moorish or pagan one – even if there were no ships sailing from this coast, but only a catamaran, I would confidently go on it, placing all my hopes in God." The catamaran he mentions was no more than a glorified raft of tree trunks lashed together, not the powerful modern vessel with its parallel hulls. He found a small ship, set off at the end of August and described the passage as follows: AFTER – "What between storms and pirates I encountered many dangers. I remember one in particular: our ship of 400 tons ran before a violent wind for a league, and during the whole time the rudder was scraping the ocean floor. Had we struck a rock the ship would have gone to pieces, and had the depth decreased at any point we would have been stranded. Then did I see strong men weeping out of fear for their lives. We learnt that our only strength comes from God and we were made to realise only too well how frail we are."

Two surprises were awaiting Francis at Malacca. The first was the welcome he received from the people, who had somehow heard of his achievements in India. A large crowd of various nationalities and ages flocked to the quay when the arrival of the ship was announced, to greet the 'holy father' about whom they had heard many wonderful things. The impression he made on one small European boy was remembered for many years: "The father beckoned to us boys, greeted each of us by our own name, and asked us how our parents were. He had never seen us before, and there were quite a few of us – no one had told him our names – he could only have known them miraculously" (the boy became a good friend of Francis and later became a Jesuit himself).

Francis spoke of the other surprise: "In Malacca I was given many letters from Rome and Portugal, and I received and am still receiving so much comfort from them that it seems to me that though I am here, I am also there, if not in body, at least in spirit." He went on to remark that his favourite relaxation was frequently to think of his friends and remember the years when they had been together in Paris, or Venice or Rome. It was in his loneliness that he fully appreciated what they all meant to him. At the end of his reply he wrote, "In spite of being so far away, I am immensely happy in my work: God gives me so much grace and comfort that I often cry out, 'Enough, Lord enough, I am not worthy of all these favours'."

Malacca, a notable port in Malaya, had previously been under Hindu, then Muslim rule. In the early sixteenth century it had been attacked, captured and fortified by the Portuguese. Its inhabitants were of many races, including a class of Eurasians (half-castes, bred from marriages between Portuguese men and Malayan women). Francis had expected only to change ships here, instead he had a three-and-a-half months stay.

He needed every minute of it to care for the Portuguese alone, for there was only one other priest in the city, responsible for the military in the fort. The civilians, without a priest for years, were rapidly losing their faith and the practice of the Commandments. Instead of publicly denouncing their evil conduct, Francis used all his talents in winning their hearts, and then gently encouraged them to repent.

He naturally gave priority to the sick in the hospital, having a little cell nearby. He succeeded in reconciling soldiers with inhabitants of the city, and started a sort of evening prayer by going through the city ringing a bell and calling people to pray for the souls in Purgatory. He had his own way of spending the rest of the night; we can get some inkling from the official who shared this bamboo cell: "I used sometimes to spy on him (through the partition) in the middle of the night. It was always the same scene – Francis on his knees, arms uplifted before a little crucifix made of wood from the shrine of St Thomas. Beside the small table, the only piece of furniture, lay a long black stone. When I watched him at last lie down he used the stone as a pillow. Then he would be up before dawn to say his Office and his Mass."

One more occupation, which cost him much more labour, was learning another language, for Tamil spoken in southern India would be of no use in Indonesia. This time he wanted to be ready with translations before he set off. Luckily for him, Malayan was generally understood in all the islands he would be visiting – even though some had one or more languages of their own (one had 14).

CHAPTER 7

The Spice Islands

When Francis left India he was expecting to go to the Macassar islands, thinking that there was a great opportunity to spread the Christian Gospel in that area. Yet he never reached them. Whilst he was waiting at Malacca, the captain of the city told him that they now had enough priests for the Macassars, and that Francis would find much better opportunities if he went a further 400 miles east to the Moluccas, popularly called the 'Spice Islands'.

Indonesia consists of a long chain of islands running south-east or east from Malacca: Sumatra and Java, north of Java there is an assortment of smaller islands; covering 400 miles, the Moluccas, some of which are uninhabited. From Malacca to the destination, Amboina, the distance is 1,750 miles and involves crossing the equator twice, once soon after starting, and again near the end.

In his letter Francis mentions only one particular danger. "There are constant earthquakes out here, and similar commotions under the sea: earthquakes are alarming enough, but not as bad as seaquakes. If you are on a ship in one of these, you feel as though the vessel has struck a rock. Many of the islands have mountains which cast forth fire with a noise greater than any artillery on earth could make, and with the fire are thrust out huge masses of rock. It is as though God is permitting Hell itself to open for the confusion of unbelievers and their vices." The ships passed through the South China Sea, the Java, Flores and Banda Seas. At the end of six weeks the captain and pilot began to fear that they had travelled too far east. Yet there was no going back because of the strength of the wind. However, Francis told them to keep calm, assuring them that they would sight Amboina the next day. They did, for on the northern horizon appeared two rocky promontories joined by a sandy neck in the rough shape of a horseshoe.

Besides Amboina there were a number of nearby islands, each with a Portuguese garrison of nominal Christians, as well as a native population who had received the faith nine years earlier, but had lapsed through lack of priests.

From Amboina Francis wrote to the Jesuits in Goa, "The island is from 25–30 leagues in circumference, well-populated and with seven villages of Christians. Immediately on arrival here (mid-February 1546), I visited villages and baptised a large number of children." It seems that the number was 400 in two months. Even to reach the villages meant climbing steep mountains, slipping in red clay, scrambling over rocks, making a way through gigantic grasses, dodging under clove trees – constantly beset by mosquitoes and other insects. Finally, Francis would reach – in the heart of the forest – a deserted-looking cluster of native huts. The inhabitants were at first terrified at the sight of a white man, but Francis was patient and eventually a small child, perhaps, would run out

44

and dare to touch his robe. With the ice broken, Francis' friendliness won over the adults and he was able to start his round of the huts, looking for the sick, and then starting to teach the prayers which the natives may have forgotten altogether.

In the short time he was in Amboina, Francis did not convert any more villages. This was left to his successors, so that less than ten years later there were 10,000 Christians in Amboina and the nearby islands. To this day Christianity is still strong in the area, now under Dutch missionaries.

Francis' next activity as a priest must have been totally unexpected – ministering to Spanish and Portuguese soldiers and sailors. He wrote, "...After my visits to the villages, eight ships reached the island. I was kept busy for three months with preaching, confessions, visiting the sick and helping many to die well, which is very difficult to do by those who have lived with little obedience to the command-ments." For a while he was amongst Europeans and speaking their languages.

The fleet consisted of seven Portuguese ships and one Spanish. The latter was what remained of a Spanish Armada which had invaded the Moluccas. They had been forced to surrender on terms which assured them a return to Europe as prisoners. All Francis' skill was needed, especially in settling the many disputes and quarrels which inevitably broke out between troops of different nationalities, with victor and vanquished herded together. Besides, there was the dreadful state of the sick and wounded, suf-fering in body and soul, with the prospect of dying far from their native land and loved ones. Yet, how blessed they were to be helped in their last hours by such a priest as Francis.

45

Francis was worn out by it all, but the rest he needed turned out to be an unplanned one, for he had an attack of fever, which at first caused great anxiety. However, by the end of July he was fit to leave Amboina and continue his travels to the other islands occupied by the Portuguese. On these voyages he travelled, not by the kind of cargo boat on which he had come from Malaya, but by *coracora* – a much smaller craft. This was powered sometimes by oars and sometimes under sail, with two of the crew banging away on wooden drums both to help the rowers to keep their rhythm and to ward off prowling demons.

There is a well-known story told some years later by a Portuguese who claimed to have been an eyewitness when one of the boats, battered by powerful head-winds, was in great danger. Francis took from inside his cassock a small crucifix, attached it to a cord, lowered it into the waves and said a prayer for the storm to cease. It did – but not before the boat had given an extra lunge which made Francis lose his grip on the cord, so that the crucifix disappeared into the waves. To say the least, Francis was disturbed by the loss – no pearl-fishers were at hand to dive in and search. But he prayed and did not lose hope. "The following day, walking along the shore of the island he had reached, Francis and Rodriguez (the eyewitness) saw a crab come out of the sea with the crucifix held upright in its claws. It let Francis take it and made its way back into the sea. Francis received it, kissed it repeatedly and knelt in prayer for about half an hour." The episode is often called a 'miracle'; answer to prayer it may well have been, but not every answer to prayer is a miracle.

On arrival at the extremely volcanic island of

Ternate, Francis as usual went to stay at the hospital, ready to serve the sick and dying, night and day. When teaching the people, he made a point of attaching to his 'lessons' some simple tunes. These turned out to be so attractive that he spoke of the result in a letter: "Thanks be to God, that it has become the custom in this island for boys in the streets, girls and women in the house, the fishermen at sea and toilers in the plantations, to sing. Instead of vain songs, they choose holy chants, such as the 'Creed', 'Pater Noster', 'Ave Maria' and many other prayers in a language understood by all, whether recent converts or not."

Early in his mission Francis found that he had the power of knowing that an event was happening far away at the very moment when he was speaking. For instance, once at the Offertory of Mass he turned round to the people and said, "A good friend of mine, John, has died this hour in Amboina... I am now offering this Mass for the repose of his soul, so please join your prayers to mine." Ten days later a traveller from Amboina brought news of John's death – at the precise time at which Francis had announced it. More dramatic still was the washing up of the wreckage of a *coracora*. It was identified as belonging to a boat whose occupants had been drowned three days before. At that time Francis had been asking prayers for another John "who has just been drowned".

Francis was confidant that the natives of these Portuguese-occupied islands would make good Christians, if only enough priests would dedicate their lives – as he had – to this apostolate.

Some 70 years earlier, great numbers of the inhabitants had become Moslems to avoid being enslaved. They really wanted neither the Muslim religion nor slavery. Yet Francis had no illusions about the risks of going to the remaining islands. When he announced this plan, there was consternation in Ternate and a determination to prevent him sailing. His own account of the problem is: "The people are a very barbarous lot and full of treachery, they are brownish-yellow in complexion rather than black, and extremely disagreeable. There are islands whose folk eat the bodies of enemies killed in their tribal wars. When one of their tribe dies from sickness, his hands and heels are eaten, being considered a great delicacy." He gives more gruesome details of how elderly members of families might be made part of the menu at great feasts, then continues: "…Within a month I hope to go to an island where such things happen – for the people want to be Christians. You would find it hard to believe the degrading ways in which the men treat members of the opposite sex." Of another group of islanders he wrote, "It is their habit to poison anybody towards whom they feel ill-disposed, and in this way they kill large numbers. There is a heathen tribe which makes a pastime of murder, and I am told that when they can find nobody else to kill they slaughter their sons and wives. They have also slain many Christians, including priests."

In spite of all the dangers Francis did go to these islands, where he was able to carry out his usual plan of instructions and of care for the sick and dying. This was in the last three months of 1546. He summed up in a rather wonderful way how he had felt during this time: "I thought I might even go blind, not from any physical causes, but from the fact that I could not avoid weeping with happiness thinking how God was helping me and comforting me when there was no human way in which help could reach me. I had to live on hope in God, an invincible trust which he inspired in me and I thought it might be a good idea to re-name the islands, 'Isles of Hope in God'."

Francis' trust was fully rewarded, for he spent three months moving round the islands and departed unscathed, after inspiring the Christians there with some of his own hope and promising that he would be sure to send priests to live with them. The people who had been so strongly opposed to his going there in the first place were now shown to be wrong. So ended another stage in Francis' efforts to plant or revive Christianity in these far-flung Portuguese possessions.

Back in India there were already many affairs waiting for him to organise, and he might have left in January 1547 on the first stage of his journey, by ship for Malacca, but he could not quite tear himself away. He reckoned that the Lent of this year would be for many the last chance for a long time to prepare well for Easter. His final arrangements were for instructions twice daily and for the continuation of a habit he had introduced – a small procession through the streets at nightfall, with a leader carrying a lantern and ringing a bell, calling on people in a loud voice to pray for the souls in Purgatory and for all persons in the town in a state of mortal sin.

In a letter describing his departure from Ternate, he wrote, "When I was leaving the island, in order to avoid the tears of mourning of my friends, both men and women, I embarked around midnight. But, even so I failed to shake them off, as I could not conceal myself. That night of departure from my spiritual sons and daughters helped me to feel my unworthiness of their devotion to me."

CHAPTER 8

India Revisited

Francis began the voyage back to India via Amboina
so as to board a merchant ship there for Malacca. He
used the two weeks' pause for building a small chapel
of bamboo poles and palm branches, where he said
Mass, then waited for any of the 400 men on board
the ships in the harbour who wanted to come to
confession. He gave much of his time to trying to
calm down soldiers and merchants, in a state of
constant enmity towards each other. The Portuguese
at this time were ever in dispute amongst themselves
and often ready to settle arguments with a dagger.

On reaching Malacca in June 1547, Francis again
had to wait, this time until the end of the year, but he
was not unemployed. To begin with, he had the enormous joy of meeting three fellow-Jesuits from Europe,
whom he had instructed to await him in Malacca.
These were to be the first part of his promise to send
priests to take his place. The joy was mutual, for
these new missionaries were given the unique chance
of being briefed for the many tasks ahead of them by
this famous 'pioneer'. Francis had seen no Jesuits
since leaving Portugal in 1541, and the three had

come to India largely through hearing of his exploits from the letters he had sent. They brought some longed-for letters, and in their conversations they were able to brief him with fresh news of the Jesuits in Europe, especially the increase in their numbers (there were barely a dozen in all when he left Rome in 1540). In preparing the new arrivals, Francis made no bones about what they were likely to face – nothing less than martyrdom. He was right, for one priest was poisoned after only two years in the Moluccas. The trials of another included nine months on the run from pursuing Moslems, being captured, made a slave, and frequently shipwrecked. At the end of nine years he had to be sent back to India because his mind had become unhinged – he was truly a living martyr. The third priest survived for a few years, but died young, worn out.

For the previous six years Francis had badly missed the companionship of his fellow-Jesuits. Now, he must have found that the month he had with these three was a period of special happiness. Equally, their departure would have probably left him sad and lonely, wondering whether he would ever see them again.

In his letters Francis never mentions pirates, yet he must have known of their existence and he soon became aware of their presence right on his doorstep. Not long after the missionaries had left, one night a particularly fierce and daring band penetrated deep into the bay on which Malacca is situated, plundered the merchant ships there, tortured the fishermen and escaped. The real fear was that after their success, the pirates might be bold enough to attempt another raid. Whilst others dithered, Francis took it upon himself to rally the morale of the captain of the city, and more or less insist that he urgently equip a fleet to set off in pursuit of the enemy. Francis' authority was such that the counter-attack was soon planned, and ten ships were despatched to find and destroy the pirate fleet. Having got his way, the next task was to support the folk at home, who soon began to lose hope when no news came except rumours of disaster.

As weeks passed, Francis was the one encouraging the terrified populace, some frenzied with anxiety for husbands, brothers, sons, others fearful of another and worse pirate raid. However, one Sunday in December 1547, he had just finished preaching in the church of Our Lady on trust in God, a virtue he had practised so much in his own life. He paused for a few moments and then said, "My friends, you should stop weeping and raise your hands to God in gratitude: today our fleet has won a great victory and scattered the pirates." Later the same day, in another sermon, he predicted the very day on which news of the victory would reach Malacca. When the crews did return, they confirmed that the day of victory coincided with Francis' prediction. One important result of that victory was the decisive removal of danger of pirate raids for years to come.

At last, in December, Francis succeeded in sailing for the port of Cochin in southern India. In spite of his many voyages, both long and short, Francis did not as a rule in his letters describe the violence of the weather or other dangers. However, of this voyage he did give some vivid details. "On our journey from Malacca to India we suffered many dangers from a great storm, which endured for three days and three nights, greater than any I have seen on this sea (the Indian Ocean). We threw everything we could into the sea to save our lives. At the height of the storm I was putting myself in God's hands and calling on all the saints I could think of, including those Jesuits already dead, especially my dearest friend of earlier years, Peter Favre." He stressed the great comfort he felt at his prayers being answered and blamed himself for his ingratitude in the past to those on whose prayers he had relied.

On reaching Cochin, Francis' first activity was to catch the post, for January was the month for ships to sail to Europe. He spent the best part of a week on letters to the Jesuits in Rome, to Ignatius, to King John and to Simon – his Jesuit superior in Portugal who was responsible for actually choosing and sending the badly-needed priests. Francis was convinced that there were many priests in Christian Europe who would be far more useful in the Indies. The letter to King John more or less demanded that he order the local governors of the Portuguese towns to do their duty for the increase of the faith, for priests could only succeed if they had the full support of these officials. "Your Majesty," he wrote, "the spreading of the faith is on *your* conscience. Remember, one day you will be judged on whether you have done this or not – by the Eternal Judge. As Fr Ignatius used to say to me, 'Francis, what does it profit a man to gain the whole world, and suffer the loss of his own soul?'" Strong words from a subject to his King.

In the same batch of letters he mentions Japan for the first time, explaining how he had got to know about the country (only recently discovered by Europeans) and giving some details of what he had learnt about their customs. He was pondering whether in the near future he or another Jesuit should go to Japan. Meanwhile, he longed for the chance to meet Ignatius once again to ask his advice face-to-face on this and his many other problems. Towards the end of his letter he said, "When I begin to think of you all, I am unable to stop writing, but I must come to an end, the boats are waiting to sail. From Franciscus the least servant of the servants of the Society of the Name of Jesus."

Francis' next concern in India was to visit the group of Jesuits now carrying on his work amongst the pearl-fishers and the Mukhavas. He had not met these Jesuits before. There were five – Portuguese, Spanish and Italian – the youngest in his twenties, the oldest in his sixties. They enjoyed a 'working holiday' for a fortnight. The best known of this group is the Italian, Antonio Criminale, the leader, himself working with the Paravas. Francis took to him at once. To Ignatius he said, "He is a great servant of God and much loved by the Christians, Moors and pagans – not to mention by the other Jesuits." Francis composed a list of ways in which they should proceed. It included advice to strive with all their might to make themselves loved by the people, for if they were loved they would gain much more fruit than if they were despised. It was a maxim at the heart of much of his own approach and success.

Further news of Criminale came about 18 months later (mid-June 1549) – he had given up his life when he and his congregation were suddenly surrounded by Bodegas (earlier enemies of the tribe). Taken by surprise, he was pierced by lances and stripped. He could hardly stagger into the chapel, where he fell in front of the altar and was beheaded by one of the raiders. He was the first of a host of Jesuit martyrs.

CHAPTER 9

The Call to Japan

By this time Francis had made his decision to go to Japan. The country had been heard of by Europeans in the Middle Ages under the name Chipangu, an island in the high seas, possessing endless quantities of gold. Portuguese merchants had found Japanese harbours to be convenient shelters from storms, and they gradually started to trade with the inhabitants. The owner of one of the ships was a George Alvares, who happened to be a friend of Francis.

One night in 1546, in the port of Kagoshima on the island of Kyushu, Alvares had Japanese visitors to his ship. One of these was called Anjiro, who begged Alvares to take him on board as he was wanted for murder. He spoke enough Portuguese to tell his story as well as part of his past life. Alvares felt that basically Anjiro was a good man – learned and deserving sanctuary – and thought that Anjiro should be introduced to Francis. Anjiro jumped at the suggestion in spite of the distance of the voyage to Malacca (3,000 miles): this was where Alvarez had last seen Francis. On their arrival there, Alvarez did not find Francis since the latter was at the time (late 1546) far away in the Spice Islands.

Anjiro could in no way go looking for Francis but was content to wait, and meanwhile, learn about Christianity, to which Alvarez now introduced him. His was rewarded when Francis returned in late 1547, and was himself waiting for favourable winds to make his journey to India possible. A meeting between the two was arranged by Alvarez and described by Francis in a subsequent letter to Rome. "Anjiro found me and was delighted, as he had come with an eager desire to learn about our religion. He speaks Portuguese moderately well so that he understood all that I told him – and I, what he told me. If all the Japanese are as keen to learn as Anjiro, I think they must have the most enquiring minds of any people I have met so far. When he attended the instructions he wrote down the articles of faith in Japanese... I asked him whether, if I went back with him to his own country, the Japanese would become good Christians. His answer was that they would not do so until they had asked me many questions and seen how I answered them. Above all, they would want to observe if I lived in accordance with what I believed. If I did those things, then, after knowing me for six months, the king, the nobility and other people of discretion would become Christians: 'The Japanese', he said, 'are entirely guided by the law of reason'."

That is Francis writing. Anjiro's version, in part: "I felt completely under Francis' spell and gave him a long account of myself... He was so delighted to see and embrace me that it was clearly God who had brought about our meeting and I was abundantly comforted merely by watching his face." In reporting this episode Francis stressed again his desire for himself or another to go to Japan, although the voyage was known to be exposed to violent storms and Chinese pirates.

When Ignatius heard in Rome some time later that Francis had himself gone to Japan, he both congratulated him on his safe arrival and told him gently that he should have stayed in India and sent two others on the Japan mission. In Goa, however, the Viceroy, although a dying man, had no hesitation in approving Francis' project on condition that Francis would remain in the city to be with him on his deathbed.

Francis had brought Anjiro with him to Goa so that the latter could have a full course of instruction in the faith. By Whitsun 1548, he was baptised with due solemnity by the Archbishop, with the name of 'Paul of the Holy Faith'. Thus he became the first Japanese Christian.

Before Francis could make any further plans for his own journey to Japan he had to make plans for the various Jesuits who had arrived in Goa whilst he was in Malaya and the Spice Islands. In his next letter to Rome he reported, "In every region of India where there are Christians there are Jesuit priests. There are four in the Spice Islands, two in Malacca, six in south India, four on the West Coast, many in Goa, especially in St Paul's College, and four destined for the island of Socotra, which I myself visited on the way to India. There are more than 30 missionaries now in India." The college at Goa did not originally belong to the Jesuits, although Francis was pressed in his early days to take over its management. This he could not do, but he provided what help he could in the person of one of his two Jesuit companions, Micer Paul, to teach there. Later he added other Jesuits and finally took over the complete running of the college. He succeeded in having a highly qualified Portuguese Jesuit, Fr Antonio Gomes, sent from Lisbon as Rector of St Paul's.

Antonio must have been amazed when he first saw all the pupils. Imagine a fellow-Jesuit introducing him to the assembly: "Father, I present to you the students of St Paul's." In front of them there were rows of boys and young men, ranging in age from 13 to 21 years. "Surely these are the native servants?" "No, Father, in this college the natives are all the *pupils*. The purpose here is the education of members of the Asian nations." "Where do these come from?" "Many races – Malays, East Indians, Siamese, Ethiopians, Kaffirs, Chinese, Burmese." Fr Rector wondered what language they spoke. "They speak their own: I think we have 19 different languages altogether." "Is there one common language?" "Yes, Fr Rector," (triumphantly) "they all learn Latin!" "Pray, tell me what is the policy of the college?" "The students are given some religious training and then introduced to European culture, to prepare them to return to their lands as priests or catechists."

No doubt Fr Rector replied in words that he hoped would be well-received and retired to work out what to make of this episode. His decision was soon announced. The only way for the college to succeed was for it to be modelled on the Jesuit College of Coimbra, in Portugal, which he knew well. It would concentrate on European pupils, that is, sons of educated Portuguese, and prepare these to serve the Church and increase the number of Jesuits in India. Inevitably, problems followed with which Francis had to grapple in the years ahead.

Francis' next activity was down on the Fishery Coast. There a worrying rumour began to spread –

"Francis is dead!" Some surmised that he had been killed by violence, others that he had been burnt to death in one of his little huts. In Goa there was universal sorrow and consternation. Francis, though he would have accepted gratefully the chance of dying for the faith, was not dead. In fact he had just despatched two priests to prepare in Goa for going to Socotra. They scotched the rumour, and reported that he had been welcomed back by the Paravas like a hero. They had festooned the town with bunting and carried him shoulder-high into the church.

CHAPTER 10

Japan: The Journey

A visit to Japan was not included in the work allotted to Francis by the King, or the Viceroy or the Archbishop. They had asked for the Jesuits to help Christians, and natives living in Portuguese possessions, in and beyond India. Japan was not a Portuguese possession, and it was only about the time of Francis' arrival in Goa that Portuguese merchants had made the first contacts with Japan. It was the meeting with Anjiro that really fired his imagination with ideas of preaching Christianity in Japan.

Another influence was also affecting him. This was the discouragement he felt at the lax morals of the Portuguese settlers and their ill-treatment of native Christian converts. It seemed to him that his own preaching and example was largely being wasted. A fresh start in a country where there were no European settlers would have a much better chance of the faith being accepted. He announced his decision in a letter of February 1549, "I have decided to go this coming April to Japan with Cosme de Torres, a priest of our Society... The arrival of the most recent group of Jesuits has resulted in there being little need for my labours in India... I am also aware that we must soon be looking towards China, with God's gracious help."

Francis did not conceal the fact that many friends in India were appalled by his undertaking such a dangerous voyage. His reaction was one of fear at their lack of trust in God who had all pirates and typhoons under his control. Once again, Francis' gift of the virtue of hope was the answer to his critics. He went on quietly preparing for the Japanese mission.

Before leaving Goa he procured from the Viceroy and the Archbishop credential letters addressed to the King of Japan declaring Francis to be an Ambassador of the King of Portugal. When he reached Malacca on the first stage of the journey he persuaded the Captain to provide money to defray his expenses. He also obtained costly gifts for the Japanese King and his courtiers, and a set of impressive robes for Francis and his party to wear to show their importance. Last, but not least, there were all the necessities required for the celebration of Mass. Francis had already in mind a formal audience with the King of Japan: "When we reach Japan we are determined to go to the island where the King is residing and inform him of the embassy we are performing on behalf of another King, not an earthly one but the King of Kings, Jesus Christ."

The search for a ship for the voyage was complicated by Francis' wish not to be delayed *en route* for long periods in Chinese ports whilst Portuguese merchants wasted time haggling over cargoes. Eventually he found a junk owned by a Chinese, nicknamed Ladrao (the pirate), who made a handsome and tempting bargain with the Portuguese Captain to take Francis *direct* to Japan. He was helped in his decision by the threat of the Captain, that if he broke the agreement, he might never see his wife and property again! Francis wrote his last letters and embarked on 24th June 1549, the feast of St John Baptist.

Ladrao's junk – a cargo boat – was described as "lumbering, flat-bottomed, three-masted, with triple planking and huge, square sails made of bamboo lathe woven into a kind of mat". The crew numbered 200; Francis' party six – three Jesuits: Francis, de Torres and Fernandez (a lay brother), and three Japanese: Antonio, Joao (both recent converts) and Anjiro. The Captain at Malacca added one of his own men, Manuel, to make sure that Ladrao kept his part of the bargain, and to act as interpreter for Francis. There were no Christian symbols on this heathen ship, but high on the poop was the joss (idol) in its shrine, on which Ladrao always relied for guidance concerning what to do next, or how to cope with the unexpected.

The route is easily described: from Malacca they sailed south-east along the coast of Malaya, turned east to negotiate the narrow and dangerous straits of Singapore, then north-east, and finally, north into the South and East China Seas up to Japan, some 3,000 miles away. As they worked their way along the coast of China, they had to put in at various ports and harbours for supplies and extra tackle (for stormy weather). Ever on the alert, Francis thought he noticed the crew slowing down and showing signs of settling for a long stay in this area. Their activities in worshipping the idol, and their casting of lots, offering of incense, lighted candles, sticks of sweet-smelling wood, might foretell good weather, in which case the crew hastened to move on. If the answer to their devotions was interpreted as an omen of bad weather, there was hesitation and dragging of heels. Even so, Francis wrote that by and large Ladrao was an honest fellow all through the voyage – the only defect he could find was that Ladrao was a heathen.

After about a month of sailing, the idol became much in demand on the day of a mighty storm. Ladrao had to drop anchor and ride out this storm. Francis described what followed: "Our Chinese companion, Manuel, happened to be passing by the hatch of the ship which had been carelessly left open. Because of the high seas the ship lurched so violently that he could not keep his balance and fell right down into the hold. We all thought that he was dead from the length of his fall and the large amount of water in the hold. God our Lord, however, did not wish that he should die. He remained for a long time with his head and half his body under the water, and for many days he suffered from a serious wound he had received on the head. After we had brought him up from the hold, with great difficulty, he remained unconscious for a long time. God our Lord was pleased to give him back his health." However, the storm had not yet done its worst. Francis continued, "While the storm was still raging and the ship being tossed about, a daughter of Ladrao happened to fall into the sea. Because of the wild waves we could not save her, and thus she drowned near the ship before the eyes of her father and the rest. The tears and lamentations were so great during that day and night, that it was most pitiful to see the great misery in the souls of the pagans, and the peril that threatened the lives of all of us who were on board. After this the pagans continued to offer great sacrifices and feasts to the idol, slaying many birds. When they cast lots to find the reason for the death of the Captain's daughter, the lot came out that she would not have died if our Manual, who had fallen into the hold, had died himself."

When the storm subsided they sailed on and within a few days reached the islands lying off Canton, in China. Ladrao had lost heart, but Francis urged him to sail on, at least to the next harbour. As they approached the entrance they were hailed by a ship coming out, which warned them that it was full of pirates. Ladrao thus had to stay at sea, and, as the monsoon was still blowing from the south towards Japan, they safely reached it on August 15th, the feast of Assumption. Francis summed up their arrival: "God's last favour to us was to steer the Captain to the very home port of Anjiro, Kagoshima, on the southernmost island of Japan. We were greeted with great love by all, whether Anjiro's relatives or not, in Japanese fashion – no handshakes, embraces or salutes, but bows of various types, according to etiquette."

CHAPTER 11

Japan: Landfall

What did Francis see as the ship sailed in? To quote a modern writer: "As they approached the harbour at the end of a landlocked bay, passengers and crew saw it dominated by a majestic volcano, puffing gently on its own island. Opposite, on the mainland, at the foot of a range of low green hills, lay the myriad thatched or tiled roofs of the city. Around were the paddy-fields and terraced groves of cherry and orange trees on the ash-covered flanks of the volcano. Francis would have been entranced by the appearance of the people – small, slight men, often tattooed by light-blue dragons, and small, demure women in graceful kimonos."

The Anjiro family house was a wooden 'bungalow' with a grass-thatched roof and many sliding partitions instead of doors and windows. The three Jesuits will have shared the guest-room, in which there were no beds, but thick quilted mats for mattresses, a blanket and a round wooden pillow. The rooms were heated by bowls of burning charcoal, and there were no chairs. One had to kneel and then sit back, with knees together, on the heels, whether for reading, writing, eating or conversing. Francis must have been introduced to the 'tea ceremony' – but he did not like tea. He found ordinary meals were taken kneeling at small, low tables, using chopsticks even for rice. He noted that the Japanese ate elegantly and manipulated their food so dextrously that not so much as a crumb fell from the plate to the table.

For the moment Francis did not write back to his brethren in Malacca and India as there were no ships sailing south till the monsoon was over, in November. He had more than enough to do in learning Japanese. As he very gradually learnt, he put into writing, for Anjiro to translate from Portuguese, the teachings and beliefs of Christians, to be passed on partly by memory, partly by being read out to enquirers. Inevitably, it was slow work. He said later that it had taken him 40 days to memorise the Ten Commandments in Japanese. In the translation, there was a fair amount of hit-and-miss, which was not clarified for some years. One Basque, speaking imperfect Portuguese, was dictating to one Japanese also speaking imperfect Portuguese, a serious explanation of the Christian faith, with no language expert to advise and check him.

Sponsored by Anjiro, the Jesuits were received by the Japanese with courtesy and interest. No doubt Anjiro had begun by giving them glowing accounts of Francis's treatment of himself in Malacca and India, and of the renown he had gained wherever he went. Before looking to introduce the Jesuit to the general public, Anjiro gathered his many kinsmen and friends, and, says Francis, "He preached to them day and night, being instrumental in bringing his mother, wife and daughter, together with several relatives and friends, both men and women, into the

Christian fold. As the majority of them could read and write they readily learnt the prayers."

Soon the powerful local Daimyo (ruler) summoned Anjiro to his castle, where he asked many questions about the teachings of the new arrivals, was satisfied with all their answers, and showed especial pleasure in seeing a picture that Anjiro had brought for him – a very devotional Madonna and Child. "The Daimyo prostrated himself before it," wrote Francis, "and adored it most reverently, and bade his courtiers to do the same. Afterwards the picture was shown to his mother, who marvelled to see it and showed the greatest pleasure... She herself also asked to have in writing a statement of Christian belief." This Daimyo seems to have had no difficulty about the Christians speaking in public, and he may well have used his authority to provide the Jesuits with a house of their own, where they could pray and work more peacefully than in Anjiro's crowded home.

By now they would be feeling the Japanese winter, still clad in light cotton clothes they had worn in India and Malacca, fifteen degrees further south. Francis, writing about further recruits for Japan, stressed that they must be well-provided with clothes made of Portuguese wool, and come well-shod, for the three of them were dying of cold. This was not surprising, as they had to endure winds and snow sweeping down from Siberia.

Learning Japanese was a long, drawn-out toil for Francis (his companion, Fernandez, was much more adept), and he felt the frustration: "At present," he said, "we are like statues amongst people who speak and converse about us a great deal, whilst we stand by, uncomprehending. It falls to us to become like little children in order to learn the language." On another problem, Francis commented that one of their blessings in disguise was the impossibility for a European of ruining his health by over-eating: "Japanese subsist on a little fish, rice and wheat: there are plenty of vegetables and some fruits, but they use these sparingly; yet they are marvellously healthy, and we, too, are in excellent health of mind and body." The Jesuits also experienced in some degree the blessing of persecution from the behaviour of the Buddhist 'bonzes' (monks), who were mostly hostile to Christian teachings and showed this "not in word only".

However, some Japanese did appreciate the courage shown by the Jesuits in their difficulties, for they knew how to admire genuine goodness and sincerity. One 'Abbot', recalling his meetings with Francis, remembered, "He was not really able to explain Christian teachings to me through his ignorance of Japanese, yet his mere presence, his face, his character and his obvious sanctity, preached better than his words the truth of his message."

When he did feel ready to start, Francis' method was to enter the precincts of a Buddhist monastery, to squat on a more or less public terrace and to read the Japanese version of his book on the Christian faith. Passers-by might either laugh, or mock, or show sympathy, or on occasion be genuinely moved. One of the latter immediately accepted the message, became his first convert (Bernard), and stayed by his side for the remainder of his time in Japan. Later, at his own request, he was sent to Portugal, there joined the Jesuits, studied in Rome in the lifetime of Ignatius, returned to Portugal, but died there all too soon. Reminiscing about Francis to the Roman Jesuits, he is quoted as saying, "For seven months I slept in the same room as he. He took only a very little sleep, during which I often heard him sigh and invoke the holy name of Jesus. When I asked him why he sighed like that in his sleep, he answered, 'I don't know, I was not aware that I sighed'. With my own eyes I have seen Fr Francis deliver many sick people from their maladies. He would make the Sign of the Cross over them or sprinkle holy water, and they would be cured."

Another convert (Michael) was the steward of a Samurai in a castle near Kagoshima. Francis inspired the latter's wife and daughter and many retainers to become Christians. Michael was shown by Francis how to baptise and became leader of a small Christian group which survived long after Francis had left. It was 11 years before another Jesuit, Br Almeida, visited the castle. He received a joyous welcome from Michael, now an old man, who asked many questions about Francis (then nine years dead), still a living memory in Michael's heart. All this time Michael had been gathering the Christians together weekly and using prayers which Francis had written for them.

The same Br Almeida also found a third convert of Francis. She was Mary, Anjiro's daughter in whose house the three Jesuits had lived in Kagoshima, and she had kept a small group going there, so that Br Almeida found 200 who were either Christians or wanted to be baptised. He was unable to stay after the baptisms, but when he returned over 25 years later, he found Mary still faithful, but the others lapsed. She had held out against the behaviour of the bonzes, but was afraid that when she died her relations would bury her in a common Buddhist graveyard. Happily, towards the end of her life, the Jesuit superior of the flourishing community of Nagasaki arranged to bring her there and so she ended her days surrounded by the love and veneration of both Japanese and European Christians. She was laid to rest with a rosary around her neck, given to her by Francis.

CHAPTER 12

Seeking the Mikado

The encouraging start at Kagoshima did not last. The
bonzes soon lost interest in the novelty of the visitors
from the outside world, and Daimyo's hopes that
Francis and his companions would promote trade with
Portugal, in such desirable objects as guns and
gunpowder, were disappointed. However, Francis'
enthusiasm did not wane. He seized the chance of
moving to the territory of Hirado, north-west of
Kagoshima, ruled by a more friendly Daimyo, already
on good terms with Portuguese merchants. This move
would also bring him closer to the abode of the Emperor.

Francis judged that he could leave his original
converts in the care of Anjiro until there might be
another priest available, and he set off with Fr Torres,
Br Fernandez, Bernard and Anjiro's original companions. There was such sadness amongst the small
number of Christians at their departure. On his side,
Francis' separation from Anjiro was for good. It was
a dramatic moment, since their first meeting at
Malacca had been the cause of Japan coming into
Francis' life, and Anjiro and his family had been the
first Japanese Christians.

The missionaries spent the summer (1550) in Hirado where they made about 100 converts, including their host, by name Kimura. This man's grandson was to become a Jesuit lay brother and 60 years later be martyred for the faith at Nagasaki. After a few months, even though winter was approaching, Francis with a few others started for the capital, Miyako, on what was to be the worst of all his journeys. Torres was left in charge of the converts at Hirado.

The route was 500 miles to the north-east. Francis said little about the journey, and it was left to Fernandez to stress some details in an account given after Francis' death to a new-arrived companion. "There are no beds in Japanese inns; at most, straw mats and wooden pillows. Arriving at one of these places in the evening, we were more than once turned away, and refused even a little shelter, although we were frozen to the bone and famished with hunger. On other occasions, when striving over rough mountain tracks, we were overwhelmed by fierce snow-storms and icy winds. Our legs swelled up under us and we collapsed where we stood; we were poor, badly clothed and obvious strangers. At some villages we were given a welcome frostier than the air, for the children ran after us yelling insults and pelting us with stones.

"During our march I watched Father with my own eyes and was deeply moved by the way he prayed as we trudged along. Meditation and contemplation were to him the most familiar of things: for all the time of his prayer he never once raised his eyes from the ground or glanced around, he kept his arms and hands absolutely still, only his feet moved, and they too, very gently. It was the same in the inns, which were little better than stables: though weary from walking, he was so gentle and humble in manner as he ate his meagre meal that you might think him a slave" (the meals consisted of a little boiled rice, some salt-fish – boiled or fried – and a tasteless soup which smelt abominable).

Eventually, bedraggled and half-starved, they came to Yamaguchi, the second city of Japan. They did not intend to stop and preach, but they were forced to wait for a suitable way of continuing the journey, which had to be done in armed company owing to the prevalence of bandits. Francis soon made Christians of the husband and wife who ran the inn where they put up. Francis and Fernandez preached in the streets without any licence or permission. Fernandez did the talking whilst Francis stood beside him praying. Fifty years later, an old man who had been baptised as a boy by Francis, remembered him as "…a man comely and spirited, who did not know the language of the country, but spoke through an interpreter, and then his countenance became suffused with blushes and glowing."

Fernandez also told of the day when they were summoned by the Daimyo who controlled 20 of the 70 provinces of Japan. "The Daimyo received us very benevolently and asked many questions about our voyage, and about India and Europe, and wanted to know about the 'Law' which we were preaching. Francis made me read from our notebook the account of the creation of the world, and the Ten Commandments, which we had translated into Japanese. After dealing with idolatry and other aberrations there followed a section on the abomination of unnatural vice. In the book it is said that men who practise such things are filthier creatures than animals that wallow in the mire. When I read the passage, the Daimyo appeared to be thoroughly enraged by it and showed his anger in his face. However, we were then signed to go, and we left without him saying a word. As for me, I was afraid that he might order our head to be chopped off then and there."

Eight days before Christmas Francis, Fernandez and Bernard set out on the next stage overland. Fernandez remembered that the snow came above their knees, and that the icy, paralysing water of the mountain streams through which they had to wade often reached their waists. He added that Francis at times went the whole day barefoot, and in the evenings at the inns he could be seen looking in astonishment at his swollen and torn feet, which had left tracks of blood in the snow.

Next, came a short, but equally cold, sea journey, with biting winds, against which they had no protection – and also biting words from the scoffing of young merchants. At the last port of call they were befriended by a rich Japanese who worked out a plan for them to complete their journey. He found a place for the three men among the servants and mounted bodyguard of a nobleman proceeding to Miyako in a palanquin. The bearers went at a trot, each carrying on his back a share of the great man's baggage. All three appear to have again gone barefoot through the deep snow for the two-day journey. Francis had acquired some sort of Siamese cap or turban and he went wearing this out of sheer good spirits, every now and then leaping and skipping like a frolicsome child. He had brought an apple with him, and this he would sometimes throw into the air and deftly catch as it came down.

So they came to Miyako, or Kyoto, as it is now called. The Emperor of Japan was the Sun-God, the

Mikado. Francis thought of him as he had been accustomed to think of the King of Spain, the King of Portugal, his ancestors the Kings of Navarre or the Viceroy of India. These gave orders and they were obeyed. After all, he had been sent to India by the King of Portugal, and sent to the pearl-fishers by his Viceroy. He naturally expected that the Emperor of Japan's permission to preach would be decisive. The unhappy truth was that although the Mikado was greatly revered, he had no power, no authority, no influence and little money. All these had been taken away by powerful Daimyos in different parts of the country. Francis did not gain an audience, since he could not find the necessary money.

Realising now that the Mikado was only a figure-head, whose "permission to preach" would have been worthless, Francis wasted no more time in Miyako, but cut his losses and returned to Yamaguchi, whose Daimyo, truly a man of great power, was much more likely to grant the necessary permission.

CHAPTER 13

Japan: A Fresh Start

It was mid-winter, and for security reasons the three Jesuits travelled by sea in an open boat where they could hardly move a limb to keep themselves from freezing. They arrived back in Hirado four months later to be greeted by a relieved de Torres. On the icy journey Francis had not yielded to disappointment at seeing that his great desire to bring the Gospel to 'pagans' had failed again. Rather, as ever strengthened by his unfailing trust in God, he started working on his next plan.

So far, he had not used the assortment of robes and gifts with which he had been provided by the Captain of Malacca. Now he would approach the Daimyo of Yamaguchi with all this paraphernalia. An audience was granted, and Francis, with Fernandez, Bernard and others, arrayed in outfits of an ambassador and his train, entered. They advanced past the assembled courtiers to present themselves to the Daimyo with both gifts and the documents. The latter were illuminated letters of greeting, from the Viceroy of India (King John's representative) and the Archbishop of Goa (representative of Pope Julius

III). The gifts included objects until then practically unknown in Japan: a grandfather clock which chimed the hours day and night, a musical box, an elaborately-worked musket with three barrels, two pairs of spectacles, various pictures in oils and an unstated quantity of port wine.

In Francis's own words, "The Daimyo in his delight offered us all sorts of things, and a large amount of gold and silver. We declined any of the gifts, and asked only one favour – that he would give us permission to preach the law of God in his territories, and allow those of his subjects who wished, to embrace it. He willingly granted this… and at the same time made over to us for a dwelling an unoccupied Buddhist monastery. There we held forth twice a day to a large crowd of visitors."

In the next few months about 500 Japanese became Christians, many of them of the Samurai class, who had at first been most opposed to the teaching of Francis and his companions. Rapidly, Francis found that the daily sessions, as well as constant summonses to the houses of nobles and others, left no time for praying, celebrating Mass, nor for eating or sleeping. Questions and arguments went on for days, with Francis bombarded from morning to night. Enquirers were especially worried by the eternal problem, "If God is all good, how can he allow evil to exist?" Francis does not give his answer in detail, but does say that the questioners went away completely satisfied.

One day as the preachers noticed with some concern that the number of converts was falling off an unforeseen event occurred. As Fernandez was holding forth, a rough-looking man broke through the crowd and spat full in his face. His response was simply to wipe the spittle off and continue his words

– a gesture which so impressed a man up till then hostile to Christian arguments, that he sought out Francis and begged to be prepared for baptism. From this time on the numbers picked up again and they included another striking individual.

It was a man who was by occupation a 'wandering minstrel', and made his living by singing at street-corners, or exercising his wit in reciting ballads and legends in houses of noblemen. His ungainly appearance concealed an acute mind, always searching for the meaning of life, and tantalising Francis with highly intelligent questions. What satisfied him as much as the answers was the love of Francis for his mission, shown by his travels through thousands of miles of danger and hardships. He was inspired to give up clowning and storytelling, and offered himself to help Francis in his labour. Baptised Lawrence, he was employed as a catechist and interpreter and in due course became a Jesuit brother. Then, in spite of his lack of education he evangelised his country for the next 30 years, using his native wit and skill in attracting the attention of others to silence the arguments of the bonzes.

During this successful period Francis was actually invited by another ruler, the Daimyo of Bungo, 60-odd miles away, to come and visit both him and the Portuguese merchants who used to put in at his port. Jumping at the chance, Francis hastily summoned de Torres from Hirado to come and take charge at Yamaguchi. He himself, with three Japanese Christians, went to Bungo and received a warm welcome from the Daimyo and the Portuguese, who included an old friend from India, Duarte de Gama. Francis soon began to win over the inhabitants (the Daimyo took many years more to accept Christianity).

During all the recent months Francis had not put India out of his mind. Indeed, he had become gradually more anxious over the complete absence of news, especially as he had left behind at Malacca careful instructions how to send letters on to him (he did not know that war and weather between them had all but cut off Malacca from Japan). Feeling that he ought to attend to his original task, the needs of India, and that he could do so and return to Japan within 12 months, he arranged with Portuguese merchants to take him back as far as one of their trading stations off China, in the hope that he would find a boat there to take him on his way to Malacca and India. He sent the long-suffering Fr de Torres a message about these plans and his intention to return within the year, together with enough money to build a small church and house in Yamaguchi.

Now, however, there came another twist in their affairs, for de Torres himself sent news that a rebellion in Yamaguchi had put him and the other Christians in peril of their lives, as they were held responsible for the troubles by their preaching against the gods of Japan. Providentially, a devout Buddhist and his wife who were also sympathetic to Christianity gave de Torres and Fernandez every possible help, hiding them first in a pagoda and later in their own home until the attacks subsided. Then de Torres went on the counter-attack, asking for a renewal of leave to preach, and for another monastery to replace their burnt-out one. His anxiety abated, Francis continued to prepare for his journey in spite of the reluctance of the Daimyo of Bungo, who had learnt to appreciate his worth.

Some time in September 1551, Francis, Bernard and three other Japanese Christians set sail in a

Portuguese ship. In no time they encountered a typhoon which Francis himself did not mention – the account of the survival of two of the sailors is only known from another passenger. The two Muslim sailors had been put as crew in the ship's long-boat, with adequate provisions as a precaution against the ship itself having to be abandoned. Ironically, it was the long-boat and its crew which came to grief and vanished in the worst of the storm. All aboard bewailed this loss except Francis. "Lower your sails," he said, "and stop mourning – I'm going to pray that God will restore the boat and the men. You will be cheering their return within three days." After he had taken himself to prayer, the men and the boat reappeared and Francis' next task was to respond to the men's desire for baptism.

Without realising it, or intending it, Francis had said farewell to Japan for good, after only two years' labour, and just when the prospects were most promising. He reached Sancian, an island off the Canton estuary, where he had the good luck to meet another old friend, Diego Pereira, waiting for a favourable wind to sail back to Malacca on his ship, the *Santa Cruz*. Pereira was distressed by a letter which had been smuggled out of a Chinese prison from one of a group of Portuguese captives who had been seized and held as pirates, since trade with the outside world was strictly forbidden by the Chinese authorities. The writer said that the only way he and his fellow victims could gain their release was for Pereira to have himself sent to the court of Peking as Portuguese Ambassador so as to bring influence to bear on the Chinese.

Francis read the letter, digested it and thought he saw in its suggestion a way of getting into China. This was an ambition he had formed early in his days in Japan, for if only (so his mind ran) he could find his way into China, get the ear of its ruler and proclaim Christianity there, then all his work in Japan would automatically succeed, such was the awe with which the Japanese regarded the Chinese. As he and Pereira made their way down the coast of China back to Malacca in the dying days of 1551, the two of them laid their plans: Pereira would be Ambassador and Francis his secretary!

CHAPTER 14

China Approached

On his arrival at Malacca in early 1552, Francis found awaiting him a letter from Ignatius, giving him the official appointment of 'Provincial' of the Jesuits in India. By this position Francis was no longer dependent on Simon Rodrigues in Portugal for the despatch of new missionaries. It now became his own responsibility to acquire fresh manpower, and his authority derived directly from Ignatius in Rome (the title 'Provincial' is abbreviated from 'Provincial Superior', i.e. the 'Chief' of Jesuits in a particular area).

In virtue of his new powers Francis now had many decisions to make and problems to solve when he reached Goa. It will be remembered that the needs of India were the reason for his leaving Japan in the previous year. He had, for instance, to reorganise the college in Goa; there were fellow-Jesuits to be appointed to various parts of India and beyond; a number of Jesuits had to be dismissed from the Order because of their unsuitability. The making of some of these decisions caused him to say that all the other sufferings and sorrows of the previous years could not match the anguish he experienced during these months in India.

He looked for comfort in waiting for a reunion with fellow-Jesuits. On their side, they were impatient for the arrival of Francis in Goa for many had never seen him. They assembled at the college, some 50 in all. Some years later one of them wrote, "Impossible to tell what joy the arrival of Francis amongst us caused." Another was more enthusiastic: "What fire of love for his neighbour, what charm! Always laughing, his face cheerful and serene. He always laughs, yet he never laughs, for his cheerfulness is all spiritual."

Amongst the Jesuits in Goa there was much holy rivalry over being chosen to accompany Francis to China. He settled on four, although not all were Jesuits. The two Jesuits were Fr Balthasar Gago and Br Ferreira; the others were Antonio, a Chinese who had been at the college for eight years (so long that he had forgotten his own language), and Christopher, a Malabar Christian who would be Francis' personal attendant. Also travelling for part of the journey was the Japanese Ambassador to the Viceroy – he was a Christian and was making his way back to his own country.

Francis had persuaded the Viceroy to agree to the plan that Pereira worked out in order to secure entry to China – namely, Pereira as Ambassador (of King John of Portugal) and Francis to act as his 'secretary'. He was given official documents to hand over to Pereira in Malacca; he had also the Papal 'brief' which he had brought with him at the beginning, recommending him to "the King of Ethiopia and other Princes of the East". Together with these documents he had been given a magnificent array of gifts for the

King of China (in Malacca, Pereira was on his own account amassing another set of gifts as well as fitting out his ship, the *Santa Cruz*, at his personal expense).

Maundy Thursday (1552) was the day fixed for departure. During the previous days Francis gave his fellow-Jesuits nightly farewell talks "...of such grace and power that they inflamed all hearts and transformed them into something new". He also wrote a last long letter to Ignatius: "We are going to the court of the King of China, which is near Japan, an extremely large land, inhabited by a very gifted race and by many scholars. Take special care to recommend us to God. Your least son, and furthest exiled..." Probably, by the time Ignatius read this, Francis was already dead. Certainly, Ignatius' last letter to him never reached him for it was dated 1st June 1553. In it Ignatius ordered Francis to return to Europe so as to report in person on the affairs and needs of the East.

At his departure from Goa the omens seemed good for Francis, but he himself was ill at ease, and showed this by hinting that his fellow-Jesuits would not see him again, and openly stating that he felt in his bones that Satan would be active in spoiling his plans – he could not guess how. On arrival at Malacca some weeks later he soon found out.

Authority in the city was shared between two brothers, Pedro and Alvaro da Gama. Whilst Pedro, Captain of the Citadel, supported the expedition to China, Alvaro, Captain of the Sea-coast, (i.e. of the movement of ships in and out of the harbour) opposed it. He stated openly that the best available person as Ambassador to China was not a "mere merchant like Pereira" but a member of the ruling-class; in other words, himself. His official position

84

enabled him to prevent Pereira's ship from sailing, if necessary by the simple action of having its rudder removed by force and impounded. It was useless appealing to the Viceroy – he was some thousands of miles away – Francis' rank as *Papal Nuncio* was scorned, especially as he could not produce the 'brief' of his appointment, as it had been left behind in Goa. Francis himself was insulted and threatened by a mob stirred up by Alvaro.

In the end, Alvaro having placated the mob, and still being in control of the *Santa Cruz*, made a compromise. The ship carrying Francis and his party could sail with a crew picked by himself (Alvaro), but without Pereira. Yet, no Pereira meant no Ambassador, so that Francis' diplomatic entry into China would not be possible. All he could now do was to sail off to one of the Portuguese ports-of-call near the Chinese mainland. This turned out to be the island of Sancian, some 100 miles south of the mainland city of Canton (and within sight of the mainland itself).

Before leaving Malacca, Francis wrote a sad letter of farewell to Pereira, blaming his own sins (and those of Pereira) for the failure of their plan: God did not want it. Francis also stressed his genuine grief at the financial losses which Pereira had incurred in fitting out the expedition, and ended by saying that he would not try to meet him again, since it would cause him so much pain.

CHAPTER 15

Francis Fails

Announcing his safe arrival, in October 1556, Francis wrote that Portuguese and Chinese merchants dealt with each other on the island, and that the former had done their best to persuade one or other Chinese to land Francis on the coast of China. None would agree because of the risk to their lives and possessions if they were found out smuggling in a foreigner. The letter went on: "I was introduced to a 'distinguished' man, a resident of Canton, who undertook to transport me and put me in the way of gaining access to the governor of the city, all this in exchange for a substantial quantity of pepper" (which the merchant could sell for a good profit in China).

Francis was not deterred either by the thought that the Cantonese might not keep the bargain (and simply abandon him on a deserted island) or by the prospect of being caught and subjected to the same torture and imprisonment as had befallen the Portuguese, whom he and Pereira had originally hoped to rescue. But he did fear a much greater danger: this was, abandoning trust in the mercy of God, for whose love and service he had taken on the mission to China.

This made him determined to get to China by any way whatever.

The original four members of his party had now been reduced to two: Fr Gago had been diverted to Japan (as Francis was not at all sure exactly when he might himself return there), and Ferreira had been sent back to Goa, since his health had become too bad for him to carry on. Francis was not idle during the weeks of waiting for his transport. He was able to celebrate Mass every day in a small hut (which he called a church), and to give himself, as in the past, to looking after the sick amongst the crews of the ships at anchor off the island, hearing their confessions and reconciling their enmities. Further, he was already thinking of alternative ways of reaching China. For instance, he happened to know that the King of Siam sent a yearly embassy to the Emperor of China: so, if he could get to Siam he might become a member of one of these missions.

So far, Francis' health had held up: back in Goa he had said that he had never felt better physically. He now had fever for a fortnight, but he recovered and was able to write what turned out to be his last letters, in which he said, "If it is the will of God, I shall not die, though it is a long time since I felt so little inclined to live as I do now." He took the opportunity of making an offer of much more pepper to the Cantonese, but there was no response.

As November dragged on he was suffering more and more from extreme cold, malnutrition and lack of shelter. These, added to the dreariness of the wait, caused him to fall ill again. There was really no suitable place on the island for a sick man, so his companions suggested that he should be moved to a berth on the *Santa Cruz* – at least he would be out of the cold and discomfort of his hut. However, one night on board was enough, for the rolling of this ship made him more uncomfortable than the icy winds (the *Santa Cruz* was the only ship left at Sancian – its Captain would not sail back to Malacca until he had seen Francis set out on the way to China). Francis was found a slightly less chilly hut, and at his own request was bled. However, this caused fainting, followed by nausea. The fever increased, as did the pain. Even so, he showed great patience.

His Chinese host now fixed a crucifix on a pole opposite the bed and in the intervals of his delirium Francis fastened his eyes on it. As far as his speech could be understood, he was repeating the names of the dear Jesuit companions of the old days back in Europe, thus showing again the loneliness he constantly felt at being separated from them. He prayed with colloquies in various languages (including his native Basque), all the time with joy on his face. At one stage he lost the power of speech for three days, recognised no one and ate nothing. Conscious again, he went on with his prayers for two more days. The faithful Antonio realised on the night of December 2nd/3rd that he was near death, and he put a lighted candle in his hands. The end came after a short struggle towards dawn, when "with great repose and quietude" the soul of Francis Xavier began its next and last journey.

He, who had so often been at the bedside of the sick and dying, died without the sacraments of the Church, or anyone to offer Mass for his soul, or even recite the prayers for the dying. It is touching to realise that in his last hours he was tended to by a member of the race which he had set his heart on evangelising.

It was Antonio who later described Francis' last days and death. His account continued, "In death the blessed Father looked so happy and so fair that one might have thought him still alive… I went at once to the *Santa Cruz* to obtain the vestments and all else necessary for his burial." Next day, a Portuguese and two slaves helped him to prepare the body, make a coffin and dig a grave. When about to fill it in, one of the party suggested that later there might be a move to transfer the body (i.e., the bones) to India; would it not be wise to hasten the process of decomposition? This they did by packing a quantity of lime above and below the corpse; they then buried the coffin and filled in the grave. Antonio arranged some stones to distinguish it from the graves of others (merchants and seamen) who had died on Sancian.

Weather kept the *Santa Cruz* in harbour until mid-February 1553, when preparations were made to sail back to Malacca. Antonio thought that in the two months since the burial the lime should have done its work, and he pleaded with the Captain to have the body exhumed. When they opened the coffin they saw that the lime had *not* worked: the body was completely intact, without giving off any odour at all. Then the Captain somewhat reluctantly agreed to take the incorrupt body on board, as long as the coffin was securely nailed down. The passage took a month, being briefly halted at a port-of-call whence word was sent ahead to Malacca with news of Francis' death and the imminent arrival of his remains.

It was Pereira who planned the welcome – an enormous procession to the church of Our Lady: this was followed by a solemn Requiem and the burial of the body, without the coffin, in a grave near the high altar. There it might have remained, in full contact with the earth, indefinitely, but for the arrival from the Moluccas of a fellow-Jesuit, Juan de Beira. On hearing the account of the death and burial he felt a great desire to look on his friend for one last time. He enlisted the services of Pereira to have the body exhumed by night. On venerating it, still unchanged and appearing as though Francis was asleep, de Beira became convinced that Goa should be Francis' final resting place.

Again Pereira took a leading part, secretly moving the body to his own house, placing it in a worthily adorned coffin and looking after it. It was December before the ship bearing the remains could leave for India, over the seas traversed so often by Francis in his lifetime, and it was well into Lent by the time of arrival in Goa. Here, still greater emotion and popular devotion was shown by all manner of Christians and non-Christians.

Francis Xavier's return 'home' eclipsed the solemnity of Lent and Passion week. The open coffin was first placed in a small church. There it was observed by one who had known the living Francis well: "He looked in stature and appearance exactly as we had formerly known him, lying there in his priestly robes complete and fresh as if he had been buried only an hour ago. Under the vestments, next to the skin the body was clothed in a rich garment which the Father had taken with him from Goa to wear at his interview with the Emperor of China. Though it had been for more than a year under the earth, it was clean and intact…"

In an atmosphere more of rejoicing than of sadness, for four full days and half the nights, crowds visited the church, all wanting to touch the feet of the missionary whose holiness was now brought home to them in the form of his incorrupt body. There was a funeral, but no burial. In due course the remains were placed in an ornate shrine where they could be exposed from time to time. The shrine itself was situated in a specially built baroque 'Basilica of Bom (Good) Jesus', where it is venerated to this day.

On one occasion, 150 years later, the shrine was specially opened for the benefit of a newly consecrated Bishop *en route* to his see in China. His Jesuit escort was present at the opening and his description of Francis' remains at this time is said to be the best ever written. "The Saint's hair is black and slightly curling. The forehead is broad and high, with two rather large veins, soft and of a purple tint, running down the middle, as is often seen in talented persons who concentrate a great deal. The eyes are black, lively and sweet, with so penetrating a glance that he would seem to be alive and breathing. The lips are of a bright reddish colour and the beard is black. In the cheeks there is a very delicate vermilion tint. The tongue is quite flexible, red and moist, and the chin is beautifully proportioned. In a word, the body has all appearance of a living man."

That witness was naturally concentrating on Francis' head. An equally moving aspect of his remains is his feet. They too, have been preserved in the same state as when he was alive. A modern photo enables us to see these misshapen, battered, twisted (but still flesh-coloured) parts of his body. These were the 'transport' which carried him over thousands of miles – without letting him down, for his final illness was not one of any specific weakness in his limbs. The feet were not in themselves a thing of beauty, yet they inevitably recall the words of Isaiah, "How beautiful on the mountains are the feet of one who brings good news."

In 1622, with his canonisation, Francis became 'Saint Francis Xavier'. In a later century he was proclaimed 'Patron Saint of India and all the East', and later still, 'Patron of all the foreign missions of the Catholic Church'.

This account could end with such statistics as the estimated total distance travelled by St Francis in all his journeys, or again the estimated number he converted. Some reckoning might be tried whether he was a 'success' or a 'failure'. Of far greater value is to reflect on the inspiration he gave, both in life and after death, to others to carry on his work. A generation further on, it was strong enough to face fierce persecution (which gave Japan its first martyrs). Over the same period, in China, Jesuits, especially in the person of the Italian, Matteo Ricci, had been officially accepted in the country. The Church continues its work, now by other methods than Francis used, but with the same desire for the glory of God which drove him on four-and-a-half centuries ago.

CHAPTER 16

Farewell

Francis Xavier was not precisely the first European missionary to the East, but he was the first to make a lasting impact on India. He was literally the first to plan preaching in China. Some writers have said (as his fellow-workers in India did) that he should have stuck to his first work in India itself, and waited patiently until this had been well established before moving further afield. In his own mind was the feeling that he must take the opportunities when they came – he did not deliberately start looking for new worlds to conquer. However, he was not put off by the labours and dangers which the journeys to Indonesia, Japan and China involved, for his Basque character made him both determined to achieve the targets and prepared to pay the cost. As a companion of Ignatius Loyola, he was committed to spending his life in search of souls.

Francis had no special training, as a modern missionary would certainly have. He knew little of the religions and languages of the peoples amongst whom he worked, apart from what he picked up as he went along, but he did not let this deter him. He was insistent in his letters that learned priests were needed who could study non-Christian religions and converse on equal terms with their priests and philosophers. As we have shown, his sheer goodness, charity and humble life drew people to him and his message much more successfully than his halting attempts to teach in their languages.

Francis' great strength came from his life of prayer, both as he went about the labours of the day, and through long hours of the night, when he could be alone. This gave him the trust both to tackle the enormous difficulties of facing the unknown, and to overcome the loneliness of his personal life: all through his years in the East one of his greatest trials was being cut off from the Jesuit companions whose life he had shared in the years with them back in Europe.

The letters (mentioned in the Introduction) themselves created such interest and enthusiasm in Europe, especially amongst Jesuits, that rapidly volunteers started arriving in the East, ready to dedicate their lives, as Francis had done, to preaching the Gospel of Christ. As a result, his early death at the age of 46 did not result in the collapse of his mission. Those who followed were both inspired by his example and encouraged by his prayers.

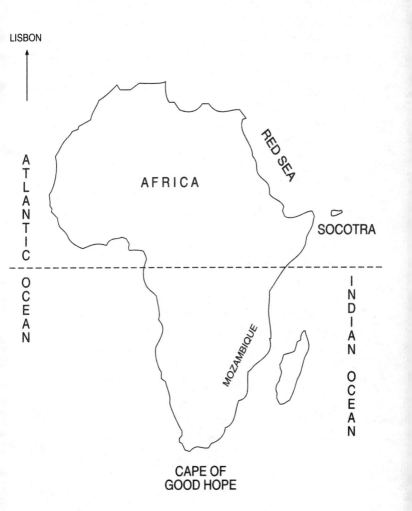

LISBON

ATLANTIC OCEAN

AFRICA

RED SEA

SOCOTRA

INDIAN OCEAN

MOZAMBIQUE

CAPE OF
GOOD HOPE